WHEN IT ALL BOILS DOWN

By Shannon M. Jefferson

"Doobie"

ACKNOWLEDGEMENTS

First and foremost, I would like to thank the Almighty God for giving me the talent and ability to finally complete my very first book. This is something I 've always dreamed of doing since I was a teenager. I would like to thank my beautiful mother, Juliette Jefferson and my father Eugene C. Goodwin (R.I.P.) for teaching and raising me to be a strong black woman. I want to make you so proud. You are my hero mommy. I love you so much.

To my sisters and brothers, Chikita, Tamika, Eugene and Troy Jefferson, along with my 4 sons and niece, Kendell, Jamel, Jaymes, Bryant and Ileah. Thanks so much for supporting and believing in me. To my brother from another mother, Drew, thank you for motivating me and pushing me to finish my book, even when it got tough. It was all a dream! To my best and close friends, and sisters from another mother, Crystal, Robin, Courtnay, LaShondra, Angel, Larry, Keitha, Quetta, Tyga and all my other family members, friends and all my supporters on social media! I love y'all so much. Thank you!

With Love,

Shannon "Doobie"

DEDICATIONS

This book is dedicated to anyone that's going through or have ever dealt with any type of physical or/and mental abuse. Any type of abuse is never okay. Get out of the situation as quickly as possible and seek help.

To anyone that's dealing with a mental illness, don't be ashamed. You are not alone. Don't be afraid to seek help. Help is out there.

Always surround yourself with positive people and keep God first. Always stand strong and believe in yourself. Everyone goes through hurt, pain and rough patches in life but it's up to you to fight through it and keep striving. You can do it. Nothing and no one is perfect. Broken crayons can still color. Always remember that.

PROLOGUE

"Oh, my God Shante', please don't do this!" Shante' couldn't believe these two. How could the two people she trusted so much betray her in this way? Her heart was damn near beating outside of her chest. With her black & silver, 9 milli-meter Smith & Wesson in hand, she pointed the gun from her and back to him.

"Just shut up! How could you do this to me? To him? To our family? How could you hold such a secret when you've witnessed the heart ache and pain that I went through after losing him? You thought I didn't know about the note that he left you? He loved you. He would have done anything for you. I told you not to break his heart but you did and it killed him!" Shante' said with tears rolling down her face. "And you, turning the gun back towards him, "WHY SHOULD I LET YOU LIVE YOU SON OF A BITCH? You are the cause of all this shit that's been goin' down. With all your lies and secrets How could you do this time him?"

"I was going to tell you but I didn't know how. I didn't mean for this to happen. You gotta believe me. Shante', baby girl please put the gun down and let's talk about this. I am so, so sorry. Let's just please talk about this before you……

POP POP POP!!!

Screams rung throughout the house as she screamed at the top of her lungs as she watched Shante' released 3 rounds into his skull. "OH, MY GOD NOOOO".

POP! POP! Shante' let off two rounds into her back without so much as a blink. She stepped over their dead bodies and placed the manila envelope on the bed. Although she looked over these documents and pictures 100 times, each time the pain was unbearable. She couldn't believe what she'd done, but it was too late. What happened, happened.

She went downstairs to the kitchen cabinet and took out a wine glass. She knew the place like the back of her hand. She went into the pantry and grabbed a bottle of red wine. She wasn't much of a drinker but after the mind-blowing news and their betrayal, she figured what the hell. She gulped down her drink and poured herself another one.

She knew the neighbors had probably already called the police, but she didn't care. She wasn't running. She figured her life was already over. Too much has happened. She was losing control. She didn't want to live, so she planned on taking the easy way out. Jail wasn't an option for her. She'd rather rot in her grave than to rot in jail cell. Wiping the tears from her eyes, she then turned the gun to herself. "Lord, please forgive me!"

…. POP!

CHAPTER 1:
EYE FOR AN EYE
1987

"Now, don't you go runnin' yo' damn mouth and telling yo' aunt about our lil' meeting ya hear? Or else the next time I'ma make it harder for ya. Shit, it ain't like she gon' believe you anyway," Frank said laughing as he pulled up his pants and climbed out of Gina's bottom bunk bed.

Frank was Shante's Aunt Fay on and off again boyfriend. Whenever Shante's mother, Pamela, went to work, she would drop her, her little sister, Gina, and their baby brother Mark off at their aunt's house until she got off. Sometimes she left them there until the next day if she got off work too late.

Every chance Frank got, he would wait until Fay was in a drunken sleep, which was most of the time, and sneak into the guest bedroom where Shante' and her sister Gina would be sleeping. Mark always slept in the room with Fay.

Shante' was the oldest child of her two siblings. She was 10, Gina was 9 and Mark was 7 years old. They were very close knit. Their mother, Pamela, was a hard-working woman and very beautiful. She was short with shoulder length, sandy brown hair. She worked as an Administrative Assistant at a law firm in Downtown New Orleans. She sometimes had to work overtime at least 3 days out of the week.

Their father, Evan, was the Chief of the fire department in Jefferson Parish. Pamela and Evans met at a grocery store one day while Pamela was shopping for fruits. They sparked up a conversation, exchanged numbers and the rest is history. He worked overnight, 6 days a week. They tried to make the best life for their 3 children.

"Gina', you ok?" Shante asked, hanging her head from the top of the bunk bed they both shared. Gina and Shante' favored each other a lot. Although they had similar features, Shante' was dark skinned whilst her sister's skin was a lighter shade of brown. They both had shoulder length natural, curly hair. Shante' was very protective of her little sister, but even she was no match for Frank's touchy, feely ass. He didn't touch her as much as he did Gina', but sometimes she would also be in attendance of his little involuntary "meetings".

"No. I wanna' go home," Gina said through sniffles. Shante' climbed out of the top bunk bed and got into bed with Gina and held her close. She felt helpless against him. She hated Frank with a passion for hurting her little sister. She needed to make him pay.

"I promise you lil' sis, one day, I'ma kill him for hurting you! I betcha' he ain't gon' hurt nobody else after I finish with him. Watch!" Shante' held on to her sister. The tears flowed from both their eyes as they cried themselves to sleep.

………………………………………………………………………..

"Gina, Shante', y'all bring y'all asses on, y'all mama here to pick y'all up." Aunt Fay yelled for Shante' and Gina from the living room. She didn't have to tell them twice. They both ran in the living room like the house was on fire. Gina' ran into her mother's arms like it was the last time she was going to ever see her. "Girl, you are hugging me too tight. Go getcha' stuff so we can go home. I'm tired and ready to lay down. Shante', go get Mark," said Pamela.

Shante' headed down the hall towards her aunt's room to get her little brother. Just as she was getting closer the room, she saw Frank coming out of the bathroom in the hallway and heading to the room where her little brother was sleeping. Instead of going to the room, she made a detour and went into the kitchen. She went to the drawer and grabbed the longest and sharpest knife that she could find. She placed it in the inside of her Care Bears PJs right arm sleeve and crept slowly down the hall into her aunt's room, walking past everyone, smiling. She always wore that up to no good smirk on her face whenever she was up to something.

Peeking inside the room, she saw Frank laid out across the bed on his back sleeping. She hesitated at first about what she was about to do. But then she thought about all the nights where she would hear her little sister's whining while Frank took advantage on her innocence. That made her blood boil. This had to be done! No time to turn back now, she thought.

She tiptoed inside of the room and slowly closed the door behind her. Just as the door closed, Frank popped his head up and said, "Girl hurry up and getcha brother so I can get some damn sleep." She didn't move. She just stood there staring at Frank. "Is yo ass hard of hearing or somethin'? Ha? You lil nappy headed ass girl?" Frank said, pissed off while standing up.

Shante' walked slowly over to Frank, got on her knees and grabbed the front of his pants. She sometimes saw her Aunt Fay do this, and it drove Frank crazy. So, she decided her revenge. With her left hand, she unzipped his pants and pulled out his soft penis. She knew that for her plan to work, it needed to be hard. She'd never done this before but watching VHS porn videos sort of gave her an idea. His penis reeked of a musty smell and dry semen. He didn't even have the decency to wipe his penis off after he got his nut from his episode with Gina the night before. She thought of sucking his dick made her want to throw up, but she had to do what she promised her little sister. Payback!

She held her breath and put his member in her mouth and commenced to pleasuring him the best she knew how. She didn't have much experience, but she must've been doing something right because Frank was moaning like crazy. "Oh shit, damn, I see my lil nightly meetings done paid off ha? Damn. Suck this dick like ya' auntie ya' lil' hoe you," Frank said, grabbing the back of Shante's head while she gave him oral. She was starting to gag because he was putting his dick too far in her mouth.

Even at 10 years old, she was used to witnessing this type of action. She used to sneak and watch porn all the time while everyone else was sleep at her aunt's house, especially when Frank wasn't there. Being that her aunt always had men in and out of her house, Shante' witnessed all sorts of sexual activities. When her aunt got drunk or loaded with one of her tricks, she would sneak in her bedroom closet and peek in on her sex sessions. She was curious, but this lip service wasn't for pleasure. Maybe for Frank it was, but for her, this was personal.

"Uh, um, shit." Moans escaped from Franks mouth like it was the best blow job he'd ever received. He didn't give a damn if it came from a 10-year-old girls' mouth, to him, head was head. He was in deed, a sick son of a bitch! His ass needs to be under the jail.

Shante' looked up at him to see if he was looking. Nope. His eyes were closed shut, just like when her Aunt Fay was on her knees giving him the business. Oh, his nasty ass was on cloud 9. After seeing her chance, she slowly let the knife slide down her sleeve, letting it fall to the floor. She grabbed the handle, slid his penis out of her mouth and held it with her left hand. With all her strength and power, she took that knife and tried to slice Frank's dick clean off.

"AUGHHH, SHIT!!" Just as he let out a scream, Shante' stormed towards the door. Before leaving, she turned to Frank and said, "I betcha you ain't gon touch me and my lil' sista' no mo'! Every time you think about usin' that musty dick of yours, you gon' think of me. Ole' nasty nigga!", she said to Frank, as she smiled and ran out of the door. She left Frank on his knees holding his now bleeding package. He was screaming and crying. He was in such excruciating pain. She didn't care. He got what he deserved. He should be lucky that she didn't cut it all the way off.

From the living room, Aunt Fay let out a, "What the hell is all that damn noise?", as she heard the screams from Frank coming from down the hall. Pamela, Aunt Fay and Gina then saw Shante' walking down the hallway with a bloody knife and some blood on her PJs. They all looked in horror as Shante' placed the knife on the coffee table in the living room.

"OH! MY LORD, GIRL WHAT THE HELL DID YOU DO?", yelled Pamela. Fay took off down the hallway to see what was going on in the room.

To Shante', it was amazing how fast her aunt can run to check on that nasty boyfriend of hers, but she would never come to herself nor Gina's aid whenever Frank would creep into their room and have his way with them. She was aware of what he was doing yet she didn't try to stop him nor did she protect her own nieces from that freak. She almost wanted to cut her ass up too.

"OH, MY LAWD!", was all that was heard. Looking from her mother to her sister, Shante' said, "I told you I was gon' get him from hurting you." She then grabbed her sister's hand and walked out of the door without a care in the world. Problem solved!

"You ain't keepin' that baby, and that's that! You ain't nothin' but a damn baby yo' self lil' girl so how the fuck you gon' raise a child when I'm the one supporting yo' ass? What the hell was you thinkin' when you let that boy get you pregnant? I raised you better than that Pamela Jenkins!" Pamela's mother, Belinda, yelled at her.

At the young age of 16, Pamela became pregnant. She found out after she missed her period for 2 months and could barely hold down any food. Her mother started noticing changes in her daughters' behavior and her body was also changing. Pamela did her best to hide it from her mother, but her mother was far from a fool.

Her 18-year-old boyfriend at the time, Kenneth, decided that he wasn't ready to become a dad. He had hopes and dreams of becoming a football player. So, with the news of Pamela being pregnant, that threw him for a loop. He figured she only got pregnant on purpose to trap him. Either way, he had no plans on taking care of that baby or being with her. He had bigger plans than being a father.

"For real, mama you trippin'. I'ma keep my baby! You can't make me have an abortion. This my baby and my body. I decide what I wanna' do with it. Not you! I'M KEEPIN' MY BABY!", Pamela said to her mother at the top of her lungs. She was holding her stomach at the same time.

SLAP!! "Who the fuck you think you raisin' your voice at lil girl? Now get loud with me again in my damn house and I'ma slap the livin' piss outta' you again. Don't play with me. You pregnant but ya' face ain't pregnant. Nah try me again. Like I said, you ain't keepin' that damn baby and livin' in my house, so you might as well throw that shit out cha' mind. And if ya' wanna' keep it, go ahead and keep it. But 'cha ass can't stay here. Go live with 'cha lil' boyfriend. 'Cause I ain't raisin' no mo' babies Pamela."

Pamela stormed to her room, holding her face. She flopped down on her bed and hugged her pillow, crying tears of pain and disappointment. Why would her own mother want her to abort her baby? This was her baby; their baby. She told herself that her and Kenneth will work things out for the baby's sake.

■■■

With that in mind, she got up and grabbed the receiver from the phone on her night stand, and dialed Kenneth's house number. The phone rang 3 times before he answered.

"Hello!", he yelled into the phone. "Look, why you keep calling my house? I told you before, I ain't ready to be a daddy. I got dreams ok? And being a daddy right now just ain't one of 'em. I can give you the money for the abortion but that's 'bout it. After that, man lose my number. This relationship is over. I'm sorry." "Click". And just like that, Kenneth was out of her life.

Pamela couldn't believe Kenneth would do this to her. He was the love of her life. He'd promise to marry her once he went pro. Now that she is pregnant, he treated her like last night's trash. This couldn't be real, she thought to herself. Her sold her nothing but bullshit and lies. She had a decision to make, and she knew just what she had to do. She buried her face in her pillow and cried herself to sleep.

∎∎

"Oh mama, the light turned green. Shante' shock her mother's arm, snapping her out of her deep thoughts. Pamela drove home, daydreaming about her past. All she ever wanted to do was to be a good mother and protect her kids at all cost. The moment they stepped in the car, both Shante' and Gina filled their mother in on Franks' sexual activities whenever they slept by their Aunt Fay's house.

She couldn't believe what her girls were telling her. When she found out that her daughters were being molested right under her sister's roof, she was livid. She would have never thought in a million years that this would happen to her own children. You hear about things like this on the news, in the neighborhood, or at family function when that one drunk uncle start yapping off about the family secrets. But when it hits close to home, it hurts even more and the pain is unbearable.

"Mama, why are you crying?", asked Gina. Pamela tried so hard to hold back her tears but this hurt. She promised to never let her kids visit nor sleep at her sister's house again. Whether Fay knew of it or not, Pamela still blamed her and held her responsible for Frank's actions. Pamela knew that Frank was scum when her sister first introduced him to her. Still, she left her three children in her care so she was held accountable for whatever happened to her daughters.

When Shante' explained more in detail of what she did to Frank in the room after she walked out the house with Gina, Pamela went ballistic. To hear the things that Shante' did to Frank made her stomach turn. She stormed back into the house and beat both her sister and Frank's asses. She kicked Frank right in his cut-up dick. She vowed not to ever speak to her trifling ass sister again.

"I'm ok baby. I am so sorry this happened. Y'all don't ever have to worry about going over there again. I will just quit my job and stay home. I promise this will never happen again. I love my babies and I will hurt someone behind y'all." As they drove home,

Pamela battled with the decision to tell their father, Evan, about Frank's perverted ass. She knew Frank would be a dead man if that happened. She figured she would just keep it between her and the girls. She didn't even want to report it nor did she want to press charges against Frank. Besides, having his dick half sliced off by Shante' was justice enough. He won't be using it anytime soon she thought. Feeling that Frank got his revenge, she decided not to inform her husband about what went down at her sister's house. This will be their secret. She only hoped that it wouldn't back fire one day.

****

"Now I lay me down to sleep, I pray the Lord my soul to keep. If I should die before I wake, I pray the Lord my soul to take. Amen." Pamela then kissed her three kids' goodnight and went into the kitchen to pour herself a much needed a glass of wine. After the kind of day she'd had, she needed a drink or two.

Pamela always made sure they said their nightly prayers as a family. Well, minus Evan. Lately, he seems to be getting home later and later. She sucked it up as work; him being the Fire Chief and all. But in the back of her mind along with her God given women's intuition, something told her otherwise. Just as fast as she thought about it, she tossed that foolish thought right out of her head. Evan loved and adored her and only her. He would never step out on her; that's what she told herself at least.

"Lord please look over me and my babies. Thank you, Lord. Amen." She said a silent prayer then headed off to bed and awaited her husbands' return home from work, if he came home at all. Still, she waited and hoped, like she did every night.

CHAPTER 2:
NEW PLACES & FACES
1990

Three years after her mother quit her job, Shante' and her family had to move due to financial problems. Not only did her mother stop working, but shortly afterwards, her father was forced to retire from the fire department after being involved in an accident while putting out a house fire. They could no longer afford their nice 4-bedroom home in New Orleans East Over. They went from living in the suburbs to renting a 3-bedroom house Uptown.

"Why y'all moving?", asked Danny, Shante's best friend. Danny was like a little brother to her. He was only two years younger than her. He was the first child in East Over that played with her. They were inseparable and as thick as thieves. They even knew all each other's secrets. She told him all about the things Frank would do to her and her sister whenever they slept by their aunt's house. Danny never met him but he really hated Frank and vowed to always protect her and Gina from that monster or anybody that tried to hurt them. Although he was closest with Shante', he treated Gina and Mark like siblings too. He became close to the whole family. When he found out that they were moving, he was devastated.

"My mama said we can't afford to live here no more so we movin' Uptown. Man, I'ma miss this house, and I'ma miss you too. Our number gon' change and everything. I'ma still be calling you and stuff though. You can always come spend the night by us," she' told Danny. "I gotta' go." She gave him a big hug and watched him walk down the street with his head hanging low. Danny didn't have too many friends like Shante'. She was always nice to him, unlike some of the kids in the neighborhood. They picked on Danny because he was short but Shante' would always fight his battles. That's why he loved her so much. He called her his big sister.

"Hurry up and put these boxes on the truck. This is our last trip." Her father, Evan, ordered to her and Gina. Evan was 5'9, very handsome and muscular. He had light brown eyes and a low cut with waves. At 40, he looked damn good for his age. Although the injury at work left him with a slight limp, he was still a sight for sore eyes. He was familiar with the Uptown area so he knew his way around well. A close friend of his at the fire department told him about the house for rent and he was all over it. Besides, they only had one more week to move out of their home in the East.

As they looked out the window at their old home as Evan drove away in the truck, they were sad about having to move from their nice house to being crammed into a 3-bedroom shot gun house. Shante' would miss her friends but she was only going to be two bus rides away. She just hoped that the kids around the new neighborhood were just as friendly as the ones in the East.

****

"Hey girl, yo' mama home?", asked Joyce, Shante's neighbor and only friend of Pamela since they moved Uptown on Liberty Street a few months ago. Putting on a fake smile, Shante said, "Yeah but she layin' down and she said don't wake her up unless the house on fire." Joyce let out a laugh.

Joyce have been living Uptown most of her life. She lived four houses down from Shante' and she knew the ins and outs of the neighborhood. She knew just about everybody and could tell you all the latest gossip. She was 39 years old but had the body of a 21-year-old model. She was wine fine. She stood about 4'9, toned, very curvy, light skinned with short curly hair. Some would refer to it as "good hair". All the men in the hood lust for her, but she had her eyes set on someone else. She had a son named Tony. He was the same age as Shante', 12. He was very tall and very handsome with light brown eyes. Joyce was a single parent; or at least she was to Shante's knowledge because she never saw a man over there, nor did Joyce or Tony ever mention his father. Tony stayed to himself a lot and he loved playing basketball. To Shante', he was cool but weird. He was just too quiet for Shante's taste.

"Well, when she wakes her ass up, tell her to call me or come knock on my door," said Joyce. Shante' wondered what her mama got out of being friends with Joyce. She was loud as hell and always in another person's business. Pamela was the total opposite, reserved and quiet to a certain extent. To say she was well known and knew a lot of people, she always knocked on their door, nonstop every other day like she didn't have any other friends. That really annoyed Shante'. She became very suspicious of Joyce.

Knowing darn well she wasn't going to give her mama Joyce's message, Shante' flopped down on the sofa and started watching Show Time at the Apollo. She loved that show, especially when the Sandman came out and escorted whack ass talent off the stage. That was the best part of the show. They would come out and rub that log for good luck, knowing they didn't have a lick of talent.

Just as she was getting good into the show, the house phone rang. "Tss, this damn phone never stops ringin'," she said to herself. "Hello," she spoke into the phone sounding pissed.

"Dang, why you gotta' answer the phone with all that attitude?" It was Shante's neighborhood friend, Darlene. Shante' had met Darlene while on her way to the corner store. Darlene and her best friend, Jovita, noticed the new face in the neighborhood and had to introduce themselves. Darlene was 12, same age as Shante' and Jovita was 11. They showed her all around the neighborhood and even introduced her to other kids around the way. From that day forward, they became close friends. Shante' was happy.

"My bad, I didn't look at the caller ID box. I thought it was that annoying ass lady Joyce that lives up the street. She gets on my last nerves. Anyways, what's up? You wanna play Double Dutch or something? I'm bored. I'm just sittin' inside, watching Apollo."

"Yeah but who's gonna jump dummy? You forgot, Jovita 'cross the river by her people. They got a family reunion, a BBQ or something like that," explained Darlene. "Aww dang, I forgot," said Shante'. "Well what 'chu wanna do then?"

"Well, we thought about playing "It" but everybody said that's boring now so we gon' play this game called Catch & Get a lil bit. You down?", asked Darlene. She gave Shante' the run down about the game.

This game was well known throughout New Orleans. Get caught, and get rolled or hunched on by a boy. Oh, this game was right up Shante's alley. Hell, yeah, she was down!

"Yeah girl, who all playing though'? I hope them lil' dirty ass lil' boys from around the corner not playing. They be beaucoup musty." Shante and Darlene laughed so hard that it woke Pamela up. "Girl cut all that damn noise out shit I'm trying to sleep. And cut that TV down too."

"Girl you got me fussed at but yeah I wanna' play. Let me get my tennis shoes and I'ma meet you on Louisiana Ave." OK," stated Darlene.

As planned, they met up on Louisiana Ave. It was Shante', Darlene, 2 other girls and 5 boys from around the way. "Ok y'all, let's go!", yelled one of the boys.

Before the game even started, Shante' already had her eyes sat on one of the boys. He went by the nickname Benny. He was the cutest boy on the block and she would make sure he was the one that would catch her.

They all took off running in different directions, trying to catch or avoid getting caught. Shante' on the other hand, had other plans. As soon as she spotted Benny, she purposely ran into him. They were in the alley of an old abandoned building. "I got cha' nah," said Benny, out of breath from the chase. "Yeah, nah what 'chu gonna' do about it?" Shante' was down for whatever he had in store. Looking side to side, they both headed to the back of the house, making sure not to be seen by the other kids, or anybody for that matter.

As soon as they were in the yard, they started kissing. "Umm, you a good kisser," Benny said. He was surprised at the way Shante' was making him feel. No girl has ever kissed him like this. He wondered if Shante' had done this before with other boys. "Who taught you how to kiss like that?", he asked. "That ain't all I know how to do," she said while guiding his hand under her sundress, letting him feel on her soft ass. With his other hand, he started rubbing on her perky breasts. Before you know it, they started dry humping each other. She was getting turned on by the second. Benny couldn't believe what was happening. And he was loving it too. They were moaning and making all types of noise. You would have sworn they were having sex.

"Oh, they back there gettin' booty!" One of the boys yelled while pointing. "No, we not, stupid! And why you gotta' be loud cappin'?", said

Benny. "We just kissed. Nobody ain't back here gettin' booty. You lie too much."

Just then Darlene came around the bin to witness what was going on. "So, what ch'all was doing and how long y'all been back here?", she asked. She had the feeling that this was planned all along and she didn't like it. Not one bit and she had her reasons for not liking it. She saw how Shante' was eying Benny before the game even started. "We just got back here. He caught me. Who caught you girl?", Shante' asked.

Darlene didn't answer her question. She just said she was tired and was about to head home. To Shante', that seemed odd being that she was the one that wanted to play that stupid game in the first place. She sensed attitude from Darlene. Ignoring her, Shante' started walking towards her house, with Benny close behind.

She then faced Benny and asked, "Can you give out your phone number?". "No but I'ma give it to you. I like you." Finally making it to Shante's house, he stood on the sidewalk and waited until Shante' came out her house with a pencil and paper to write down his number.

"Here. Don't call me after the 9'0 clock props tho", he said. They both laughed and went their separate ways.

∙∙

The following Monday at school, Shante' couldn't wait to see Benny. He was in one of her 2 classes. They were both 12 and in the 8th grade. They were only a few months away from heading to high school. During the weekend after they exchanged numbers, they were on the phone Sunday for hours in that short time.

"Girl that's all you talk about now, augh." Darlene hated when Shante' went on and on about Benny. It was all she talked about ever since they played that dumb game. She hated herself for even introducing them in the first place.

"You mad, jealous or drove?", Shante' teased. "No boo, I could never be jealous. I'm just tired of hearing Benny this, Benny that. Getting on my nerves with all that." Darlene was annoyed but decided to let it go.

"So y'all two go together now or something?", asked Jovita. Darlene gave her the run down about their weekend while she was across the river at her family's BBQ cook out. Since Jovita moved on 6th Street, she had always hoped that Benny would talk to her or make her his girlfriend. No matter what she tried, he didn't budge. He would speak to her but that was about it. But now, finding out that he liked Shante' instead of her, she was becoming more pissed and jealous every time Benny and Shante' was mentioned.

You see, Darlene and Jovita were best friends before Shante' moved Uptown. So, Darlene loyalty really lied more with Jovita rather than Shante'; even though she considered Shante' as her close friend too. She knew that Jovita had a thing for Benny. That's why she was upset that he gave Shante' play but didn't give her girl Jovita the time of day. She didn't want to make it seem like while Jovita was gone, she hooked Benny and Shante' up because that wasn't the case.

"No, not really but we like each other though," Shante' said while looking straight at Jovita. She peeped Jovita rolling her eyes but she played it off like she didn't see her. She knew she was hatin' on the slick. Hell, it wasn't her fault that Benny wasn't feeling her. Not her problem, she thought.

During lunch time, the girls noticed Benny and two of his boys sitting at the table against the wall. Shante' said, "y'all let's go sit over there by them." They agreed and walked in the direction to sit with Benny and his friends.

As soon as he spotted Shante' approaching their table, he stood up to give her a hug, with the biggest smile on his face. "Hey pretty girl," Benny said while eying Shante'. "Hey you", she responded. Benny gave her butterflies every time he looked at her.

"Oh, so that's all you see is Shante'?", Jovita said rolling her eyes. "What's wrong with you?", he asked her. "You speak to one, you speak to all," she said with attitude of course. "That's right. Nigga we knew you before Shante' even moved around here. So don't act brand new with us." Darlene threw in her 2 cents.

Benny just shook his head, ignoring their sly remarks. He knew Jovita was jealous of him and Shante', but he didn't care. She was known as the "fast girl" in the neighborhood and he wouldn't be caught dead with her. He wanted a good girl; and Shante' was just that. None of the boys in the neighborhood could say they hit that. He couldn't say the same about Jovita though. For the next 30 minutes or so, they all laughed and talked until the bell rung.

Throughout the remaining of middle school months, Shante' and Benny became inseparable. When you saw one, you saw the other. Girls tried to give Benny some play but he only had eyes for Shante'. He had never met a girl like her. She was his first true love and he was hers. They planned a life together.

After they graduated middle school, Benny went away to Atlanta to work with his uncle for the summer, while Shante' got a summer job as a clerk at a gift shop at the mall. She missed Benny so much. She couldn't wait until the summer was over so that she can see him again. They talked on the phone every night, but it wasn't the same. She needed to feel him, kiss him, and see those beautiful eyes of his again. They hadn't had sex yet, but Shante' was anxious about letting Benny be the one to pop her cherry. They wanted it to be special. Besides, they were both virgins. They never went pass kissing and feeling on each other. She even went as far as letting Benny stick his fingers in her pussy. But that was it. She decided that he would be her first.

CHAPTER 3:
FIRST TIME

"You miss me for real?", Benny asked while on the phone with Shante'. It was the first week of August and it was almost time to start high school. Benny had finished up his summer work out there in Atlanta and was returning home in 2 days. Shante' was over joyed. She missed him so much. She decided when Benny returned, she would give him the welcome home gift that he'll never forget. She thought about how her first time with Benny would be. She'd heard girls in the neighborhood speak on their first-time experience. She wanted to find out for herself.

"Boy, you know I miss you. Why would you ask me that? You didn't get no lil' girlfriend on me out there in Atlanta ha?", Shante' asked while laughing. She already knew the answer to that.

"Don't play with me girl. I don't want these girls out 'chea. Besides my uncle worked the piss outta' me. I didn't have time to do shit but work. I'm so happy I'm 'bout to leave. I miss home, plus I'm ready to see you."

"Well," said Shante', "At least we get to spend two weeks together before school start. When you come back home, let's go to the Joy on Canal St. and see a movie or somethin'. Or whatever you wanna' do, I don't care 'cause I just wanna' be 'round you." Benny agreed. They talked for about 45 minutes before ending their call.

****

Dozed off on the sofa, Shante' woke up to a loud knock on the door. "What the hell?", she thought as she got up to see who was at the door. She looked through the peep hole and instantly rolled her eyes while twisting the knob. "What the hell they want," she mumbled to herself.

"Girl I see you, open the door. It's hot out 'chea." Jovita and Darlene were standing outside of Shante's door eating icebergs.

"Girl, why you knockin' like you the dog on police? And how come y'all never call before y'all just pop up at people house like that? I was knocked out."

"Well excuse me miss attitude. My bad. I didn't think we had to call before we came to see our friend. What cha' in here doing anyways? You know yo' boo come home today ha? What y'all gon' do?" Darlene asked while looking from Shante' then back to Jovita. Shante' wondered what that was all about. Her and Benny have been an item for some months now. So why Jovita was still jealous of their relationship was beyond her. She thought she'd be over it by now. Guess not.

"I was watching TV and fell asleep. Y'all down bad. Could've got me a frozen cup too." Shante' stated. "And yeah I know Benny be home today. I talked to him this morning. Girl, I think I'ma let him break my virgin."

Hearing those words, Darlene damn near choked on her iceberg juice. "You for real? You not scared you gon' get pregnant? I heard it hurt the first time too." She wondered if Shante' was for real or pulling her leg.

"I'm not gon get pregnant stupid. That's why they got condoms, duh." Darlene can be so dumb sometimes, she thought. She looked over at Jovita and noticed her attitude. "What's yo' malfunction?" she asked.

"I'm good. That's all on you and him. That's yo pussy and you can do what 'chu want with it." Shante' can tell that Jovita hated the idea of her and Benny having sex for the first time. She'd always hoped that Benny would be her first.

"Well, just be careful girl. We 'bout to go. I'ma' see you tomorrow." Darlene gave Shante' a hug while Jovita half smiled and waved goodbye. Shante' locked the door behind them and went to her room to freshen up for

Benny's arrival in a few hours. She was going to make sure she looked fly for her boo.

****

"Girl, she makes me so damn sick. If I didn't know no better, I would think she was rubbing him in my face on purpose. She knew when she first moved around here that I liked him. Why you introduced them two anyways? You know I like him Darlene. That was a stupid move on yo' part."

On the walk to Darlene's house, Jovita finally broke down about why she didn't like Shante', although she pretended to be her friend when she was around. Jovita had all the boys in the neighborhood up her skirt but the one she wanted, which was Benny, didn't even look her way twice. She hated it. Most of all, she hated Shante'.

"Don't be blowin' on me 'cause they like each other. I was just being friendly and introduced her to our neighborhood friends. All them boys you talk to, girl what 'chu mad for? If you want him for yourself then make ya' move but don't take it out on me." Darlene told her off and they walked the rest of the way to her house in silence.

****

"Gina, did you see my other red slipper I had on the other day? I can't find that sucka' nowhere." Shante' almost tore their whole room up looking for her matching slipper. "No. You looked in the closet?", Gina asked. "Yeah but I can't find it."

"Well, wear something else then. He ain't gonna' be lookin' at your feet anyways." Gina and Shante' both laughed.

Shante' put on a pair of her black sandals to match her black and red summer dress. She freshened up and used some of her mama's lotion and body spray that she got from the Avon lady in the neighborhood. She had to be dressed and smelled fresh for the special occasion with Benny.

****

"Look at you, jumpin' all shive and stuff. You look nice." Benny walked up to Shante' and gave her the biggest hug. He got home around

3pm and the first thing he did was call her. His father and mother had to leave for work so since he had the house to himself for a few of hours. He invited her over to chill.

"Hey boo, dang you got darker." Shante' was rubbing her hands up and down his arms. "If you worked in the sun all day, every day, you would be darker too. Let's watch some BET videos." Benny guided Shante' to the love seat sofa. She had to admit to herself, he was looking damn good.

They cuddled up on the sofa watching music videos and talking for almost an hour until Benny offered her something to drink. "No thank you," Shante' said looking at him. He had to cutest dimples she'd ever seen. She could feel her heart beating fast as he came out of the kitchen with his cup of water. After taking a sip of his drink, he walked over to her, lifted her chin up and kissed her soft lips. Their kisses felt like fireworks. Benny started rubbing his hands on her breasts. She loved when he played with her breasts. She was ready for more. Her womanhood was throbbing and after doing all that dry hunching and finger fucking for months, she was ready for the real deal. "Where your room at?", she asked while grabbing Benny's arm.

"You sure you ready for that?", Benny was just as nervous and Shante' but he damn sure wasn't going to let her know it. "Yeah, I'm ready, a lil' bit." And with that, they both walked hand in hand to Benny's room.

Once in the room, they started undressing themselves. After she got undressed and threw her clothes to the side, Shante' climbed in his bed and got under the sheets. Benny followed suit.

"Is this gonna' hurt? You not gon' use a condom? 'Cause I'm not trying to get pregnant Benny." She was even more nervous as she thought she would be. She wanted to make sure she didn't get pregnant, especially at the age of 12. Her mama would kill her and her daddy would have Benny's head.

"Tsss, I don't have none. But I'ma pull out. I promise. I don't think you can get pregnant if I do that." Benny explained. "OK," she agreed.

They kissed for a few more minutes. Shante' could feel his dick getting harder as it rubbed against her thigh. You ready?", he asked. "Yes", she said.

"Umm." Shante' let out a soft moan as Benny entered her for the first time. She was so wet and it felt so good. Benny was in heaven. "Damn girl, yo' pussy fiyah'. Benny started with slow strokes then increased once he was deep inside of her. They both moaned and groaned until Benny started shaking uncontrollably and was on the verge of cumming.

"AUGH." He couldn't control himself. Before you know it, he was pouring his seeds inside of her. He said he would pull out but the feeling was too good. Once he was done, he lay there on top of her, out of breath and sweating bricks. It was over, just like that.

Shante' wanted more, but knew she had to hurry up and get up to wipe herself and head home. It was almost 5pm and her mother would worry her whereabouts if she didn't beat those street lights.

"When we gon' do that again? And don't give my pussy away ya hear?", Benny said with authority. Having sex for the first time made him feel like a man in that short moment.

"Benny don't play with me. You know you the only boy I like. I need a towel or something to wipe myself and then I gotta' go. I'ma' call you tonight." Shante said while putting her clothes on. "Here, you can use my t-shirt." Shante' wiped herself off, got dressed and kissed Benny goodbye. After their first time, they couldn't get enough of each other. So, every time they got a chance, they had sex. And it got better each time. They bother were hooked on each other.

**CHAPTER 4:
UNWARM WELCOMING
1994**

"Ring." The first bell rung for homeroom class. Shante' was now 17 years old and a senior in high school. She has grown from a girl into a young lady over the past few years. She went from a training bra to a 36C bra size. She had a small waist with a round, ample ass. Every boy in school wanted her for himself, but she didn't give them the time of day. She was already spoken for.

Her and Benny was still a couple and still going strong. He was Captain of the football team and, of course, girls constantly threw themselves at him. She had to admit, she often wondered if he ever stepped out on her because of all the attention he was getting. She knew he only had eyes for her, but temptation was a challenge.

She still hung out with Darlene and Jovita from time to time. She also gained a best friend throughout high school. Her name was Nadia Thomas. Nadia was skinny but beautiful with caramel skin and straight hair down her back. She was from Lake Charles but lived in the city for almost 3 years when her dad job transferred him to New Orleans. Her and Shante' became friends when they had to work on a science project together a couple of years ago in their Chemistry class. From that point on, they were close friends. She was also 17, same age as Shante'.

"Shante', hey girl! What you wearing for prom? I'm still undecided girl." Darlene caught up to Shante' in the hallway. They had the same homeroom together. "Girl I'm probably gonna' wear a blue and silver dress. Something to match what Benny wearing."

"I should have known you was gonna' wear his colors." Darlene spat. "You coming to the baby shower this weekend? It's gon' be by my house." asked Darlene. "Yeah I'ma come." What is she having anyways?"

"A boy. She still trying to figure out a name for the baby though. She wanted to name him after the daddy but he ain't with that shit, she said," Darlene stated.

During the summer before her junior year, Jovita found out she was pregnant. Everyone in the neighborhood pondered about who was the father because she never mentioned a word about who knocked her up. She had multiple sex partners so no telling who was the daddy of that baby. When asked about the baby's father, she would only say, "y'all don't know him." Shante' found this odd. I mean, they were all close friends so why not spill the beans on the baby father's identity?

"Well she can't keep quiet for long because when the baby comes I'm sure the daddy will be around. So, she might as well run her mouth." Darlene spat while walking into her homeroom class with Shante'.

****

"Girl yo' ass forever reading them damn magazines." Shante' walked in her room to find Gina reading The Source magazine. That's all she seemed to do. Most of the time, she would only get the magazines for the posters to hang around their room.

"Cause they be having all types of good stuff in this book girl. You know I'ma read anything with Dre on the cover." Gina said to Shante', giggling. "So how does it feel to be graduating from high school in a few of months? You goin' with Benny to the prom sis?"

"Girl who else I'ma' go with, silly?", said Shante'.

"I'm just saying. You know all the girls be tryin' to holla' at yo' man. He might change his mind about bringing you, that's all. It happens." That thought crossed Shante's mind before, but she quickly dismissed it. They were the "It" couple. No other girl in the whole school could hold a candle to her. "Girl please. Them lil chicks don't have shit on me." Shante' said, self-assured.

"I guess you're right sis. So, you going to Jovita baby shower Saturday? I wanna' go just to see who the daddy is!" Gina was just as anxious as Shante' about wanting to know about the child's father. It was rare to see teenage girls pregnant around that time. Jovita and her baby bump was the talk of the block.

"Yeah, you wanna' come with me? Shante' offered Gina to join her. "I doubt the daddy will even show up at her baby shower though sis. Mostly girls and women gon' be there." Shante' and her sister talked for a while before it was time for dinner and bed time.

****

It was a warm Saturday, and towards the end of February. The baby shower started at 2pm so that gave Gina and Shante' more than enough time to get ready.

Shante' wore a pair of Guess jeans with a Guess t-shirt along with her white K-Swiss. Gina' wore a pair of shorts with her Adidas matching shirt and shoes.

"You ready sis?" Shante' asked her sister while fixing her hair. "Yeah, let's go." They hugged their parents and headed to the baby shower.

****

"Damn girl, you 'bout to pop." Darlene, Shante', Gina and Nadia all went to Jovita's baby shower. Darlene and Jovita's mother made sure they went all out for her best friend. They decorated the place with blue and yellow ribbons and balloons. Jovita had so many gifts for her new bundle of joy.

The cake table was amazing. "I know I'ma get a slice of that cake." Shante' loved cake.

"Thank y'all for coming. We about to get started with the games and giving away prizes. I be glad when I drop this load y'all. This damn baby be hurting all my back and stuff." Turning to Shante' while rubbing her belly, Jovita spoke, "Hey Miss Thang. So, when you gon' let Benny pop a baby in you? With all that fuckin' y'all doing, you bound to end up pregnant sooner or later." Jovita knew it was only a matter of time before Shante' ended up pregnant too.

She threw Shante' off with that statement about the amount of sex that her and Benny was having. The only person she really discussed that with was Darlene and her sister Gina. She knew off top that Gina would never tell Jovita her sister's business. So that only left Darlene. She should have known Darlene would open her mouth to Jovita about her business.

"Girl you must be stuck on stupid if you think I'm 'bout to get pregnant. My mama and my daddy would kill me. Straight up. Plus I'm trying to go to nursing school when I graduate. No time for a baby. Not to look down on you or nothin' but girl I wanna' have fun while I'm young. But I ain't gon' lie, girl the dick is good though."

They all laughed and joined the guests for fun and games. They played games like guessing the baby food flavor by taste testing and scooping up cotton balls blinding folded. Everyone had a good time.

****

"AUGHHHHHH, this hurt. I can't walk." Jovita water broke just three weeks after her baby shower. It was time to finally welcome her baby boy into the world. "The cab 'bout to come just try to stay calm girl before ya' pressure go up." Darlene advised her best friend to try and take it easy. Jovita called Darlene about 2am when she noticed her water had broken. Good thing she only lived around the corner. She got there in no time.

"BITCH, this shit hurt!" Jovita didn't want to hear "calm down". She was in pain. "Call White Fleet again please girl, I gotta get to Charity before this baby come out and they takin' forever."

"They outside now. Come on." Darlene grabber her hand. Along with Jovita's mother, she helped her friend in the cab and they were on their way to the hospital.

****

"1, 2, 3, PUSH"! Jovita had already pushed 3 times. She was one push away from entering her baby boy into the world. "AUGHHHHHHHH." She pushed using all her strength. And just like that, out came her little baby boy. Jovita was exhausted but was happy that it was finally over.

After the doctors cleaned her baby up, she held him in her arms for the first time. She fell in love with him. A tear of joy escaped her face. She knows this baby was the beginning of something beautiful.

"You got the most beautiful dimples; just like your daddy," she whispered to her baby, as she kissed him on his head before she passed out into a deep sleep while he was still in her arms.

CHAPTER 5:
SURPRISE. SURPRISE.

Pamela decided to take Shante' shopping for her prom dress. Prom was just around the corner and she wanted to make sure her girl was ready for her big day. She hated doing things at the last minute.

"Oh Shante', what about this one?" Gina grabbed a dark blue dress and showed it to her sister. The dress was indeed beautiful. It was sleeveless with silver rhinestones at the top. It was the right style for Shante's curves.

"Yes, I like this one. I'm about to try it on right quick. Thanks sis." Shante' asked the clerk to unlock the fitting room so she can try on her dress. She hoped this was a perfect fit. They'd been out shopping for a dress for a while now.

"Ma', y'all could have let me stay home with daddy, yeah. I don't like coming to girl stores." Mark said with his arms folded. He hated shopping with his mother and sisters. They took forever. Besides, he wasn't getting anything so why did he have to tag along?

"Boy be quiet. All you wanna' do is go outside and run around with them bad ass boys and those fast tail ass girls. Ya' daddy sleeping and you know I'm not letting you outside unless I'm out there with you. Your 'lil behind like to run off. We almost finished so stop ya' whining." Pamela said.

"I WANT THIS DRESS!" Shante' stepped out of the fitting room looking like a princess. It fit her body like a glove. That dress was meant just for her, she thought. Benny was going to fall in love with her all over again in this dress!

"Awwwwwww. You look so beautiful my baby. Come on. Change back so we can pay for it. We still gotta' find your shoes and jewelry."

Pamela paid for her dress and they ventured off to other stores to get everything Shante' needed for her prom. They decided to stop at a buffet to eat since they'd been out shopping all day. Once done, they were headed home.

****

"Hey baby bro, how you been?" Shante' was on the phone with her friend Danny. Since moving from New Orleans East, her and Danny has been keeping in touch a lot, and sometimes he would visit them Uptown.

"I'm good sis. Ready for the summer that's all. How you and that pretty boy ass Benny doing? Y'all ready for prom night?"

"Yeah, I just picked out my dress and stuff today. I been calling and beeping him since the day before yesterday but he never returned my calls. Must be busy with football stuff. Ya' know my baby trying to go pro ha?"

Shante' haven't heard from Benny since the last time they talked the night before last. She wondered what that was all about. It wasn't like him not to return her calls; let alone, her 911 pages.

"Oh. Well you thought about going over to his house to see what's goin' on?" Danny only met Benny twice and he thought him and Shante' looked good together. He knows that she really cared about him so he hoped that Benny wasn't dodging her on purpose. He knew that her not hearing from him really bothered her. According to Shante', that's what's been going on for the past couple of days.

"Oh no bro. I don't rock like that. My daddy always taught me never to do popcorn visits. I'll just wait til' he calls back or when I see him at school Monday." So, what's up with you and your secret lil' boo? When I'ma meet her?" Beep, beep, beep. "Yeah sis, I been meaning to tell you. I...." Before he could answer her, her phone beeped indicating that she had a call on the other line. "Hold on bro', somebody else is calling." Shante' clicked over to answer the other line. She hoped that it was Benny finally returning her call.

"Bout time I hear from you. You been missing in action lately. Girl you know Jovita had the baby ha? He is so cute girl. She still at Charity if you wanna' go see her. She asked about you," said Darlene.

"Whaaaaaaat?! I didn't know she had the baby already girl. I'ma go see her today. Let me go 'cause I got Danny on the other line. Tell her I'ma come see her today."

"Okay girl, bye." Darlene and Shante' ended their call. She clicked back over to tell Danny the news. "Hey, I'm 'bout to catch the bus to Charity to see Jovita new baby. I'ma call ya' later or if not, tomorrow. Love you bro." "Love you too sis and be careful." They ended their phone call.

Shante' got up and put on her tennis shoes. She was excited to see the baby. Before she left to catch the Freret & Tulane buses, she tried Benny's number one more time. Still, no answer. "I'ma just call him when I get back," she said to herself. She was off to the bus stop to see Jovita's new baby.

****

"He got your eyes, too. He gon' be a lil' heart breaker." Jovita said to her son's daddy. He had finally come around to see his son. He wasn't around much during her pregnancy, which made her angry, but she forgave him. He was there now so that's all that mattered to her. She would be seeing more of him now that they had a baby together, she figured.

"I know, but what you gonna' name him though? And I hate my first name so naming him after me, hell no, that's out the question," said the child's father.

"Well I want him to be a junior so I'ma name him after you. I don't see what's the big damn deal. What man don't want their son to be named after him? You on some other shit. For real." Jovita was pissed. He was pissing her off doing all that tripping about wanting to name their son after him.

****

Shante' finally made it to Charity. The ride to the hospital was horrible and the bus was so packed with people and it was beyond hot. It was usually crowded like that on a Saturday but she figured the AC on the bus must've went out or something because it felt like 100 degrees on there.

She walked into the hospital and went straight to the receptionist desk and asked the room number where Jovita was staying. The lady gave her the information and she was on her way.

Shante' was so happy and excited to finally see the baby. She caught the elevator to the 4th floor and made a right to the maternity ward. As she walked down the hall, coming up close on Jovita's room, she stopped in mid stride. Her heart was beating so fast, she thought it was gonna' explode inside of her chest. Had she been hearing things? Was her mind playing tricks on her?

"No, I must be trippin'," she thought to herself as she continued to Jovita's room.

****

"Do don't this shit no Jovita. Now you trippin'. You know you can't name that baby after me. You up here acting like he was created out of love or some shit. You knew just what the fuck you was doing when we started fuckin' around. I know yo' simple ass lied about being on the pill. If you think this baby means me and you a couple now you can keep dreaming. That baby ain't trappin' me. Ain't no telling who the daddy is anyways. Good think he looks just like me. Or else every nigga in the city would need a DNA test."

The baby father was pissed. He wasn't getting through to her. He already regrets even having sex with her. And unprotected at that. All he wanted to do was see his lil man and for them both to agree on his name. Now she was giving him a hard time about not naming the baby after him. No way in hell he was agreeing to that.

Jovita found out that she was pregnant at 14 weeks. Instead of letting him know, she decided to keep it a secret. She figured if she told him about the pregnancy, he would try to talk her into having an abortion. And that was out of the question. So, when she became five months pregnant, she finally let him know of the pregnancy and the baby was his. Of course, he didn't take light of the situation. He didn't want a baby and he damn sure didn't want one with her.

One night at a house party, they were drinking and one thing led to another. They had sex about three more times until he decided to finally break it off. It wasn't right but she'd been throwing herself at him nonstop. She started becoming clingy and annoying. It was turning him off. She wasn't his main girl. Jovita for was the block!

"Boy, fuck you! You wasn't talkin' all that bull crap when we was fuckin'! We fucked, you liked it and now we got a baby together, so get over it. I don't know why you all uptight about it now. You knew it was bound to happen 'cause you didn't have no condoms every time you got in this pussy. So, miss me with all that bullshit about me being on the pill or not. That shit ain't 100% guaranteed anyways. And please don't let this "name thang" issue be about that bitch 'cause I can care less about her ass. Ha! That fairy tale is about to be over since we got this baby together now. So, I'ma name him what I want and that's a wrap." Jovita said rolling her eyes.

"Name him after me and watch I don't sign that damn birth certificate. I regret dickin' yo' stupid ass down from the get go. You know I…"

He stopped in mid-sentence. You would have thought he'd seen a ghost the way he was staring at the door entrance. Jovita on the other hand, had the biggest smirk on her face. She was waiting for this moment. Her petty ass even started clapping.

…Benny?" Shante' said, while grabbing her chest.

CHAPTER 6:
PRESS RECORD

"I haven't made the final decision to go back yet, but I'm damn sure thinking about it girl. It's been a long time and this depending on my husband shit just ain't cutting it for me. I need my own money, plus I just miss working. Shante' is old enough to keep an eye on her sister and lil' brother now if need be. Gina ain't too much of a problem. But that son of mine is wild as hell."

Pamela and Joyce was sitting on the porch, shooting the breeze and enjoying a wine cooler. Pamela had been thinking about returning to work since the kids were older. She didn't discuss it with Evan yet but she would bring it to his attention sooner or later. She needed her independence back.

"I feel ya' girl. But you had to stay home after what happened to your girls at 'cha sister's house. But to tell you the truth, Chile you better than me. I would have killed that triflin' son of a bitch Frank and ya' sad ass sister. Last I heard, they had to sow his shit back together. Serves him right." Joyce said, talking loud as usual, as she took a sip of her drink.

"Girl don't talk about that shit right now while my husband is in the house. He doesn't know about what happened and I wanna' leave it like that. I've been able to keep them skeletons in the closet all these years and they gon' stay in there." Pamela expressed to Joyce.

"Girl my bad shit I didn't know he was home. He must be invisible 'cause I never saw his ass the whole time y'all been staying out here. But back to Frank's ass, I'm just saying. You shouldn't have kept that type of stuff from your husband though. I would've told him. Frank would be one dead mutha fucka if it was up to me. So, when you plan on telling him about you wanting to go back to work?" asked Joyce. Just then she spotted Tony heading their way, bouncing a basketball.

"Hey mama, hey Ms. P.", he spoke while kissing his mama on the cheek. "Boy, you smell like sweat and outside/" Both Joyce and Pamela laughed. This was something they always said to their kids when they came inside.

"He got a part time job at a factory but he still getting disability and retirement pay. He works at the second shift and sometimes he works overnight so he sleeps all during the day. You'll meet him eventually. I'm thinking about giving Shante' a graduation BBQ so I'll introduce him to you then. But girl, that boy of yours is getting taller and taller by the day. Joyce, I been meaning to ask you, who is that child's daddy, Shaq? Yo ass is 4'9 and he is well over 6 feet tall! He must get his height from his daddy." Pamela was curious. Joyce never really mentioned his father much and she never saw her with a man.

"Yeah girl, he gets his height from his daddy side of the family. I don't talk about his daddy much 'cause his ass wasn't in Tony's life. As far as he knows, his daddy dead and gone. He still looks out for us though."

Joyce had an on and off affair with Tony's father. She loved and worshipped the ground that man walked on. One problem; he was married and had a family of his own. She begged him over the years to leave his wife to be with her and their son, but he would always tell her to wait a little longer. He said that for so long that is sounded like a skipping record to her.

She had so much animosity towards his wife. She was the reason they couldn't be a family. Sure, he'd send money for his son, even paid her bills, but he wasn't ready to leave his family for her just yet. He wanted to wait until his other kids were a little older. Child support would be a pain in this ass if he left then. So, with that, they decided to slow things down for a while, until he files for divorce or separation, if ever. They still maintained some contact in the meantime. She was done playing the fool and the hidden woman. She still loved him. No denying that. So, she decided to wait.

"Mark, come here right quick. You want another wine cooler?" Pamela yelled for Mark to bring her another drink and offered Joyce another one. "Yeah I'll take one." Joyce excepted.

They sat on the porch for a couple of hours and parted ways because it was time for Pamela to prepare tonight's dinner. She decided to fix Yakamein. Her kids loved it.

Just as she started boiling the water for the pasta, she heard Evan coming in the house. She headed to the living room to great him. He sat on the sofa and turned on the TV.

"Hey baby, we need to talk," she said while giving him a hug. "Ok." Was his response.

"Well, I been thinking about going back to work. You know, since the kids are older and all. How do you feel about that Evan?"

"It's up to you baby. I don't know why you stopped working in the first place. But if you wanna' go back to work, you got my blessing." Evan responded without taking his eyes off the TV.

Pamela was happy. The conversation was smooth sailing. "Well let me get in here to start this food baby. And thank you for understanding." Pam kissed her husband on the lips and he smacked her ass before she headed to the kitchen.

"Man, y'all nasty." Mark turned his nose up at his daddy after seeing him smack his mama on the ass. "Boy how the hell you think yo' big headed ass got here. Go get me a bear son. Make yourself useful."

Mark got his dad a beer and headed to his room to use the phone. He dialed the number and waited for her to answer. "Hey, what's up beautiful?"

"Hey yourself." She responded. "Yo' sister know you be calling me? You know how she gets behind you."

"Man forget her. Y'all the same age so you don't owe her explanation. So, when you gon' be my girlfriend? You got my nose wide open and shit."

Mark and Nadia talked on the phone for 45 minutes until his mother called him down for dinner.

****

She went into her bedroom closet and searched for a spare tape to make a copy. She put the tape in her 2-sided cassette radio. On one side she pressed play, while on the other side, she pressed play and record at the same time. It was like music to her ears.

She wanted to make sure she had a copy of her recording. One day, it will come in handy. When the time was right. "Like a malt to a flame." After the taping was done, she kissed both the original and the copy tapes and placed them on the upper shelf in her bedroom closet.

CHAPTER 7:
HEARTBREAK

"Shante', hold up!" Benny yelled for Shante' to wait while he catches up to her. He was caught off guard when he saw her walk into the room while he was talking to Jovita about their baby. He knew he was caught, red handed. He was going to tell her eventually but he didn't want her to find out this way. He'd begged Jovita not to mention anything to Shante' about it. He wanted to be the one to break the news to her himself. He should have known her grimy ass wouldn't hold water, but he can't fully fault her though. They both did damage control from messing around with each other behind Shante's back in the first place. He only hoped that she would forgive him. He loved her too much to lose her. Especially to a low down, dirty bitch like Jovita. He cursed the day he even let that scallywag taste the dick.

"Baby, please. Let me talk to you." Benny pleaded with Shante' as he grabbed her hand. "Look, I was gon' tell you but I just didn't know how baby. Please believe me. I didn't even know she was pregnant 'til 'bout 4 months ago. She said it was mine but I don't even know if I'm the daddy. He does have some of my features, but that don't mean shit. Anybody could be his daddy baby you gotta' believe me. I never meant to hurt you like this Shante'."

"What is there to talk about Benny? So, is this the reason you been duckin' and dodging my damn phone calls and not returning my 911 pages? 'Cause you been laid up with that bitch and now y'all a family and shit? You telling me somebody else might be the daddy doesn't soften the blow. The point is, YOU WAS FUCKING HER!"

"Not to mention, you knew for 4 months that you could possibly be the father of her baby, yet you still failed to mention it to me? Why Benny? Wasn't I enough for you? You know, I could have dealt you with fucking some random bitch off the streets that I didn't know. Sure, I probably would have been pissed the fuck off but I would have forgiven you eventually and we could have worked it out 'cause I love you that much. To fuck with this scandalous ass bitch, who I really thought was my friend is one thing, but to have a baby with this hoe? Benny, I can't compete with a baby. Every time I see that child I will be reminded of how y'all two muthafuckas' fucked clean over me. And I'm sure than sure that that bitch would make my life a living hell! No. I can't do this with you Benny. You made your bed with that dog hoe, now lie in it."

Getting on his knees, he begged and pleaded for her forgiveness. "I'm so sorry. I don't want that girl. We got drunk at a house party Downtown and she came on to me baby. I swear. We messed around that one time and that was it. She been sweatin' a nigga behind yo' back. You know that girl been after me since we were in middle school."

"You know you the love of my life and if I can take it all back baby, I wouldn't have given that bitch the time of day. But if that is my seed you know I'ma have to be around her and it's killing me already thinking about it. I know I sound selfish but I still want you around, even if this is my baby. I can't lose you Shante'. Please think this over. Don't just throw away what we had. We can fix this."

Just as Benny finished talking, the hospital room to where Jovita was staying swung open.

"Oh, so you ain't gon' tell her about all the other times we fucked around? Don't try to down play the shit Benny. You know what's up. We fucked way more than once so don't sit up here and act like I forced you to fuck me. Nigga you gave me the dick willingly. Tell her the truth. Yo' stupid ass already busted. No sense in lying now!"

Jovita stormed out of her room with her hospital gown half way off her shoulder, eying Shante'. If looks could kill, Shante' would be a dead bitch if it was up to her.

She'd just overheard Benny and Shante' in the hall way. She wasn't about to let him drag for her when it was more than one time that they'd had sex. "So now you know and yes, he is the daddy!", she said with folded arms.

"Since we were little, I always knew you was a dog bitch. Fucking and sucking every nigga that blinked his eye at yo' ass. But I considered you my friend. What, you couldn't get him with your heart so you threw some pussy at him instead? I'm not surprised at all. Hoes like you use what ya' got cause that's all you got. You a tired hoe and gon' always be a tired ass hoe. That baby ain't gon' slow you down. He got a hoe for a mother!" Shante' was so pissed off, she wanted to make sure her words stung.

"Call me whatever you want boo boo, but yo' nigga liked it. That's right. You thought you had him on lock ha. Yeah he gave me some of that good dick you used to always brag to me and Darlene about. What you thought I wasn't gon' try to test the waters for myself? Well, mission accomplished. Even if I did have to be conniving to get it. He damn sure came back for more. So, what does that tell you? You knew from day one that I always liked him, and you went behind my back and started fucking with him. And on top of that, you started rubbing the shit in my face. Now look who's lookin' stupid now?", Jovita throw back at Shante's, laughing in her face.

Before you know it, Shante' hauled off and started punching Jovita nonstop in her face. Benny tried to stop her, but she had the strength of 10 men. He'd never saw her like this and he knew he was the cause of them fighting. "Y'all stop, baby, let her go!"

By now, Shante' and Jovita was going at it, punch for punch. Even though she had just given birth and didn't have all her strength, she was still holding her own. Still, she wasn't a match for Shante'. She took all her stress troubles out on her ass. She was getting the best of Jovita.

Just then a security guard ran down the hall and broke up the fight. While being dragged back into her room, Jovita yelled out to Shante', "Fuck you bitch! Don't get mad 'cause I fucked yo' nigga. Who mad, jealous and drove now, bitch?! Don't let me catch you slippin' Shante'!" Jovita spat at her.

Shante' didn't respond. She just turned around to leave as Benny grabbed her from behind, hugging her waist. "LET ME GO!" Tears were running down her face uncontrollably. The love of her life and her so called friend had betrayed her in the worst way. No way in hell she was gonna' forgive him and take him back. The damage was unfixable. She was broken hearted.

"Let me go Benny! Go be with that bitch and her baby. Y'all low down muthafuckas can have each other. Fuck her and fuck you." And just like that, she was done with Benny.

CHAPTER 8:
DECISIONS & ULTIMATUMS

"I am writing this letter to you in good faith my love. Or however you take it. Shit, I really don't care to be honest. But go ahead, read on.

I have been waiting and waiting for you to move forward with our plans and yet, nothing has changed. You don't love her but you still don't wanna' leave her. Meanwhile I am left waiting in the dark like some type of hidden fool. I mean, how the hell does that make any sense? How long do you expect me to wait until you finally decide to grow some balls?

Well, I'm tired of playing these fucking waiting games with you! This shit feels like watching paint dry. Time is steady passing and I am sick of waiting. So, let me help you speed up the fucking process. Either you tell them, or I will. I don't have time for this bullshit. I've waited in the dark far too damn long and frankly I am tired of this down low bullshit! I deserve to be happy too. What about my happiness?

See, you men are a trip and a half. You think you can go and toy with our feelings and emotions, and act as if you don't have a worry in the world. Floating around the city with your little wife and kids, yet I have to sleep alone every damn night and I can't even have a man of my own from waiting on your ass to make somethin' shake. You think I got time for this shit? Waiting while you live your life? You got the game fucked up, darlin'. It's time I nip this bullshit in the bud.

Just in case you don't get the picture, let me make this shit perfectly clear for you, when you get this letter, so will she, along with all the proof of your infidelities. Let's see how your precious little wife is gonna' feel knowing she married a cheating ass, lying bastard. You can't have your cake and eat it too darlin'.. Not when it comes to my time and feelings.

You put us on the back burner long enough. I played my part, now it's time for you to do the same. I'm sick of you pulling at my heart strings without any remorse. I'm calling all the fucking shots from here on out! If I gotta' grab you by the fucking balls to make you man up, then so be it! Do what the fuck you need to do and don't play with me. Handle your business. And mark my words, don't ignore my warnings. That would be the WORST mistake of your life! I told you, I love you, to death!"

After proofreading the letter, she folded it and put it in the envelope. She placed the letter, an envelope with the copies of DNA results, pictures and a cassette tape in a postal service box. She smiled as she took a pull of her cigarette.

She didn't want to send the package off right away. She wanted, no she needed to add a little more salt to his wound when it came down to it. She knew just the perfect time to do so. The timing wasn't quite right just yet. Only if she could be a fly on the wall when the package reached its destination. Lives will be changed, and hearts will be broken. But she didn't give a damn. She was tired and deserved to be happy, too.

****

"Ms. Jenkins, the doctor would like to see you now," said the receptionist at the women's clinic. The place was packed with wall to wall women that day. Some were pregnant while some were there with their babies and little kids.

Looking around the waiting room area, she really hoped that she didn't see any one she knew. She didn't need anyone questioning why she was there. Especially for her reason for being there. It didn't matter though, she had to do what she had to do.

As she walked to the back room, she wondered if she was making the right decision. After all, she did still love him. Although he hurt her so bad. This could have been one of the happiest days of her life. Instead, she cried endless tears about everything that took place in that hospital a few days ago. To her, he forced her hand after what he'd done to her heart.

"Right this way, Ms. Jenkins," said the doctor, leading her into the room. "Are you aware of the precautions of this operation? I just want to make sure that you fully understand the mental and physical outcome, once it's done. Was this your decision or were you forced into making the decision?", asked the doctor.

She nodded and spoke, "yes, I am sure and I made the decision on my own. It's just not the right time. Let's just hurry up and get this over with, please."

"Alright then. Carefully read over these documents, sign and date. When you are done, change out of your clothes and into these gowns. Then lie down on the table. I will be back shortly." With that, the doctor left out of the room to give her time to get changed.

She couldn't stop herself from crying. This was it. She had to go through with this abortion. She didn't want to bring a child into the world like this, being heartbroken and betrayed by the one person she loved and trusted so much. Besides, he'd already fathered a child with her back-stabbing friend. She didn't bother to tell anyone of her pregnancy since she'd decide not to keep it. She only prayed for forgiveness.

"Ok Ms. Jenkins, just lie down and relax. Are you ready?"

"Yes, I'm ready," said Shante'. She then closed her eyes as tears rolled down her face while she heard the vacuum suck away the life of her unborn child.

"Forgive me."

CHAPTER 9:
GREETINGS

"We are one, and that's the way it is, we are one." Franky Beverly and Maze blared through the speakers. The DJ was doing his thing. Everyone was looking and feeling good and dancing to the music. Today was Shante's big graduation BBQ. The upcoming Friday was her graduation so her parents decided to throw her a big party.

Her neighborhood friends, classmates and family were there. Everyone was having a good. The food was delicious. They had chicken, ribs, hot dogs, deviled eggs, sandwiches, dirty rice, pasta, along with boiled crabs, shrimps, crawfish, potatoes, corn, sausages and turkey necks. They went all out for their daughter.

Although Shante' appreciated her parents for throwing such a special event, her heart just wasn't into it. She still dealt with the heartache of Benny and Jovita messing around behind her back and creating a baby. Plus, dealing with the aftermath of her abortion was too much for her. Still, she wore a smile because she didn't want to seem unappreciative. Her parents spared no expense on her party.

She didn't even get to go to her prom. On the night of the senior prom, Benny showed up at her doorstep, dressed in his prom suit with flowers for her, but she ignored him. He constantly called her every chance he got. She wasn't ready to hear his voice nor was she ready to see his face. She hoped he didn't show up at her BBQ. And she hoped like hell that bitch Jovita didn't show her party, either. If she did show up, she was gonna' mop the floor with her ass again.

"Girl, why you over here with the stank face? This is your party. What's wrong boo?" Nadia was concerned about Shante'. "Girl, I just got a lot on my mind. Still undecided of what I wanna' do after graduation. I wanted to go to nursing school but I'm not feeling that anymore. Might take my ass to the military or something."

"I hear ya. I feel the same way. The pressure is on now friend. Decisions, decisions. By the way, have you heard from Darlene since Jovita had the baby?" Nadia noticed that Jovita and Darlene haven't been around lately.

"Girl, fuck them backstabbing bitches! I don't consider them skanky ass hoes as my friends no more. How the fuck you knew Benny was fucking Jovita and not even tell me? Yet you steady smiling in my face like it's all good. See that's the reason I don't befriend a lot of females to this day. Hoes be trifflin' behind your back yet be smilin' all in your face. Beaucoup scandalous." Shante' was beyond pissed. She knew that call from Darlene telling her to go to the hospital to see Jovita's baby was all part of their plan.

"Yeah, that was foul. You gon' be alright. It ain't gonna be you stuck with a baby at a young age, missing out on life and opportunities. That's what she gonna' have to do eventually 'cause I heard she dropped out of school and everything. Her mama 'nem damn sure ain't helping her ass. As for Benny, I can't even believe he stooped that low. Jovita, really? Every nigga 'round the way done hit that nasty pussy hoe. I swear boys these days only think with their dicks. I'm saving this pussy for when I'm married."

They both laughed. After talking with Nadia, Shante' felt a little better. She always kept it real with her and told her what she needed to hear. That's what she respects the most about Nadia, plus she was a loyal friend. When Shante' went through her heart break and betrayal with Benny and Jovita, she was there every step of the way.

"Wassup lil' mama," Mark flirted with Shante's friend Nadia. Mark was growing into his own. He was now 14, tall, very handsome, on the basketball team in school and had his dad's charming looks.

"Hey yourself." Nadia flirted back." She was very attracted to her friend's little brother.

"Boy, leave Nadia alone with yo' young ass. My friend don't want you. You still wet behind the ears," Shante' teased. Her lil' brother Mark always had a thing for the older girls. Nadia was only 2 years his senior, same age as Shante'. On the low, she had a lil crush on him, too. She enjoyed their secret phone conversations. His age really didn't matter to her.

Mark was fine and all the girls threw themselves at him. So, she didn't mind him flirting at all. She liked it attention. She thought it was cute.

"Man, why you cock blockin' sis. Let me holla' at cha friend if I want to. Dang. Stop hatin'," he said nudging Shante'.

They all laughed and joined the rest of the party.

****

"Girl, you really did your thing for Shante'. I'm enjoying myself. You got some fine ass family members too girl. Umph. Might leave here with one of them fine muthafuckas tonight. Shit, I got cobwebs down there girl, that's how long it's been since I had some good ole fashion lovin'." Joyce was scooping the crowd at the BBQ.

"Girl, yo ass is crazy. And that is TMI. But yeah, I got a big family. Thanks for coming girl. I was starting to think yo' ass wasn't gon' show up. I called ya' three times with no answer. Glad you made it though. I know yo ass wouldn't pass up on a good time plus free food and drinks." Pamela laughed.

"You know I wasn't gonna' pass up on shit that's free. I love to party honey! I was just at home handling a lil' business. That's all. You know I had to come and support Shante'." said Joyce, smirking.

"Pamela, where is the other seasoning for the crawfish?", Evan yelled over the music to Pamela. "I'm coming baby. Come with me in the kitchen Joyce. You finally get the meet my husband." Joyce followed her to the kitchen with her drink in tow.

"Honey, this is my friend Joyce. And Joyce, this is my husband Evan. Mr. Invisible that you spoke of." Pamela introduced the two. "Nice to meet you Joyce." Evan spoke while shaking Joyce's hand.

"Girl I see why you been hiding him all this time, he fine as hell!" Joyce was intrigued by Evan's good looks. Pamela gave Evan the seasoning and excused herself and went into the bathroom. Evan double checked to see if Pamela was in earshot of what was about to transpire.

"What the fuck are you doing here? Are you serious?! How do you even know my wife and how do you know where I live at Joyce! You should not be here damnit! What the hell is yo' problem?" Evan barked.

"You may wanna' lower your damn tone for one thing. What, you didn't know I was gonna' do my homework and find out your whereabouts? Who do you think helped to find the house you are now living in? You best believe I had something to do with that baby."

"Yeah, that's right. Fix ya' face. I know everything. I thought we agreed to ease up a bit on our relationship until you got things finalized, but I see your ass just disappeared and had no intensions on going along with our plan. Just a phone call here and there. I guess you thought that was gonna' keep me in my place ha? Look at you. You wanna' play Mr. Husband suddenly Evan? What about what we'd agreed on? You forgot about that, or you just didn't think that New Orleans was so big that you wouldn't eventually run into me again? Tuh, well think again. I can find a needle in a haystack baby," Joyce winked and took a sip of her drink.

Evan stood there, angry and confused. He wondered how she found out where he lived. He hasn't been in physical contact with Joyce for a while. He still sent her money faithfully every month and called her on the phone. In all honesty, he had no plans on leaving his family for her. She was just a woman on the side. It wasn't supposed to last long as it did. No lie, Joyce was in deed a good-looking woman, but she was too demanding and a damn nut case. She knew damn well that he was a married man when they first met. Still, she begged him for years to be with her. He did care for her; maybe a little. But he just didn't love her the way she loved him. Yet still, he stayed around and gave her broken promises. Seeing her here at his daughter's party had him beyond spooked. He figured Joyce had come just to humiliate him in front of everyone.

"Look, I told you to wait it out, give me time to do what I gotta' do. I have a family damnit and a lot of shit to lose. What is wrong with you, showing up at my house and befriending my wife, Joyce? I send your ass money every month for your bills and for Tony. So, what is it that you want from me? Right here, right now, is not the time for you to start this shit

Joyce. Not at my baby's party. We will talk about this later." He started to walk off until Joyce stood in front of him.

She walked over slowly to Evan and placed her hand on his chest. "Last I checked, this was a free country. So I can be wherever the fuck I wanna' be. Besides, I was invited, by your wife. So, I'm here. As far as your dear "wife" goes, you know, who's title you keep throwing around in my face, that bitch ain't no friend of mine. I just used her clueless ass to get closer to you. Yeah, she been telling me all about her perfect little husband and kids. I wonder what she would do if she found out you've been living a double life behind her back? Wouldn't she be surprised? Should I be the one to break the news to her today baby?

"Oh, and speaking of such, I got a surprise for you. You'll know what it is when you get it. Until then, be nice and play dumb, or else I will expose your ass in front of your family and friends. We wouldn't want that, now would we? Try me Evan. I don't give a fuck about none of these muthafuckas out here. It's me and you forever baby, remember?" She smiled while taking a swig of her drink.

Just as Joyce stepped away from Evan, Pamela came from the back with the crawfish seasoning.

"Yeah, I am happy for Shante' too. She's a smart and beautiful young lady. Y'all really did a great job raising her." Joyce said, acting as if her and Evan was having a conversation about their daughter when Pamela walked back into the kitchen. Pamela didn't notice the look on her husband's face. If she did, she would have known something wasn't right.

"Here ya' go baby." Pamela gave the seasoning to Evan.

"Nice to meet you again, Evan. I'll be seeing you around," Joyce walked away, waving while winking at him.

Outside, in the yard, unbeknownst to them, someone overheard their whole conversation.

"Well I'll be," she whispered after witnessing Joyce and Evan's little confrontation in the kitchen. She juggled whether to check him about it or not. She needed to gather more information. With that, she joined the rest of the party, while keeping a close eye on Joyce.

****

"Shante' Marie Jenkins." Her parents, family, friends and classmates went crazy when you called Shante's name at her high school graduation. They were so proud of her.

She accepted her high school diploma and smiled to take pictures. It was the best day of her life. She was so proud of herself.

"Let's all go to Ryans 'cross the river, I'm hungry." Shante' was ready to get her grub on after her graduation. After taking many pictures, they all headed to Ryan's to eat.

"I'm so proud of you baby girl. You did it!" Evans smiled from ear to ear as his watching his baby girl chow down on her food while wearing her cap and gown.

"Aww thanks daddy." She said. They enjoyed the rest of their day and headed home. Today is the first day of the rest of her life, she thought as she ate.

CHAPTER 10:
2001

"I'm so damn tired." Shante' was on the elevator, heading to the parking garage to get her car and leave for the day. She is now 22 and working as a receptionist at a law office and saving to put herself through college. She wants to major in Criminal Justice, something she has always had a passion for. She went from a young lady into a full-grown woman. She had a low, curly cut and was even more sexier than before. Even her breasts and ass filled out, and she still maintained that small waist.

Once she got to her car, she opened her trunk to retrieve her hang bag. Before she pulled off, she checked her watch to see what time it was. "I still got time to grab something to eat," she said to herself.

Rollin' down I-10, she was thinking of all the things that took place in her life. She lost all contact with Jovita and Darlene. She ran into Jovita a few times in the neighborhood and every chance she got, she rubbed Benny's son in her face. Bernard Wilson, Jr. was his name. Over the years, Darlene tried to reach out to her to plead her case, but she blew her off.

Last time she heard of Benny, he was working at a plant in Baton Rouge. Word on the streets is, Jovita was sucking him dry for money. The more he makes, the more she takes. Oh well, he asked for it the day he started fucking her. He deserves all the hell she putting him through. She gon' continue to make his life a living hell. That's all on him.

Shante' didn't feel sorry for him one bit. In her eyes, they would have been married by now with their love child or children, if it wasn't for his "slip up" with Jovita, as he like to call it. Trying to pretty it up. More like "fuck up".

Mark and Nadia was an item now. They were head over hills in love with each other. At first, she was against their relationship because Shante' is very protective of her little brother. She warned Nadia of the consequences if she ever broke his heart. Although she didn't think it would last, as the time went by, their little puppy love relationship grew on her. She even had a little 6-month-old niece, named Melody. She was a beautiful little girl. She had mom's hair and her dads looks. They are spoiling her already.

As far as her little sister, Gina, she is now married to a guy named Jeremy Roberts. She loved her sister, but something was quite off about Jeremy. She just couldn't put her hands on it. Shante' always told her sister that she thinks they got married way too soon and at a very young age. She didn't think that Jeremy was the right man for her little sister. But never the less, she still respects her sister's marriage.

Her parents were doing ok. Although lately her mother has been feeling very down and depressed. Shante' hated to see her mother like this. She felt so helpless.

Immediately after her BBQ party and her high school graduation, her father started changing drastically. Coming home even later than before, if he came home at all. They barely even talked or did married couple things like they used to. He says it's the job but he works part time and his job doesn't require him to stay out until the next day. So that excuse was a load of bullshit. All the kids were grown and moved out of the house. Still, she didn't want to be in the middle of their marital problems. She loved both her parents. She only hoped that his little actions were just a phase.

****

When Shante' pulled up to the building, the parking lot was packed. She could barely find a parking spot. "Damn I wish those muthafuckas would give employees reserved parking. This some bullshit," she said to herself. She finally found an empty spot and parked.

It was Tuesday night, and to her surprise the club was packed. That meant there was big money in the house tonight. She loved the money she was making, but she just hated those cheap ass men. And a few of the ones that paid well were either paid ballers, too aggressive or plain old weirdos. She only dealt with it because she needed the money. She had a purpose for dancing and she didn't get any pleasure out of it like most of the girls that worked there. She wasn't trying to make a career out of dancing. She just wanted to stack just enough to get her through school and she was out.

"Wassup bitch! 'Bout time yo' ass made it. Baby when I tell you, them niggas out there ready to spend that cash. Shid, a bitch like me GOTS to get paid ya heard me? I been 'bout my money." said one of the dancers.

"I hear ya girl, shit my ass almost didn't come. You know my day job be having a bitch so tired. But you right, we need this money!" Shante' hi-fived the other dancer and started to get dressed into her dance clothes.

Moments before her performance, Shante' had to take a shot of any alcohol available. Even though she has been dancing for almost a year now, she always seemed nervous right before she went on stage to dance. She couldn't face her audience sober, no matter how much she tried to leave alcohol out of the equation. It was impossible. She didn't drink outside of the club, but in the club, a couple of shots always helped calm her nerves some.

Shante was one of the top 5 dancers in the strip club. The competition was fierce but she always managed to come out on top when it comes to getting her money. She was naturally a very attractive woman. She didn't even have to take her clothes off and dudes were automatically attracted to her. Guys from all type of professions showed up to see her dance. She even had a few doctors and lawyers that broke big bread whenever she hit the stage.

One guy even came in and gave her his rent money. She wouldn't have known if it wasn't for his wife storming into the club and slapping him upside his head for taking their rent money and giving it to her. She had the nerve to demand their rent money back. Shante' laughed and walked backstage. Shit, it wasn't her problem. She worked and got paid for it. Simple as that.

"Pour a shot for me while ya' at it boo." Just as Shante' was about to take another shot of her drink, she turned and saw this dark skinned, petite but curvy chick coming her way. She had to admit to herself, she'd never been attracted to women, but baby girl had it going on. This girl was stacked. Her breast wasn't that big but she had ass for days. Chocolate skin and bowlegged. What a combo. She knew all the men would be after a new face tonight.

"Hey, my name is Fancee. I just started tonight but trust me when I tell ya', you name a strip club in the city honey, and I've been there. These niggas out 'chea ain't tryin' to break bread with a bitch but want you to do all them fuckin' tricks. By the way, what's your name beautiful?" she asked. She started smoking a blunt as she waited for Rain to pour her a shot of whatever she was having.

"I go by Rain in here, but my government name is Shante'. Nice to meet you." They shook hands and Rain' poured her a shot.

"So, how long have you been dancing here boo? You seem kinda' nervous. Don't you go on after Star?" Fancee sensed her nervousness. She can always tell when dancers still haven't gotten the hang of dancing sober. Shit, she was once in her shoes. She's been in the game so long, dancing became second nature to her. It was just like breathing.

"Girl I only been dancing a year here. I got a day job but I am trying to save so I can put myself through school. You know how that goes. I be a lil' nervous cause I hope somebody I know don't recognize me and the shit get back to my people. Nobody but my best friend knows that I am dancing here. But he cool though. He won't say nothing about it." Shante' said laughing, but she was serious.

"Girl, that's why you got that damn mask over there?" Shante' would dance with different masks so she wouldn't be recognized. A few other dancers thought it was only a one-time act. But when she came out every night with a different mask, they figured she wanted to stand out or didn't want to be recognized. They got used to it though.

"Yeah plus I like being mysterious ya know? Scorpio shit!" They both laughed. Just then the manager walked it. Her name was Bunny. She was 6 feet, caramel complexion and the body to die for. But she only liked women. She had a bad ass body but attitude and demeanor like a stud. She loved pussy just as much as those niggas out there in the crowd.

"Just the 2 ladies I wanted to see. I need y'all two to do this lil' bachelor party for one of our biggest clients. His name Jon Boy. The other bitches acting stank like they don't wanna' make this money. So y'all two are my last hope. So y'all gon' cover that for me? Trust me when I tell y'all, the money is good. Believe that. Plus, I'll throw in a lil extra for y'all looking out for me at the last minute. So, y'all down?" She asked while looking from Fancee to Shante' (Rain).

"You fuckin' well right we in! Hell yeah." They both agreed. "Alright then, it's gonna' be next Thursday at 7pm at his homeboy crib cross the river. I'ma give y'all more details next week. I really appreciate it y'all."

As Shante', laced up her heels, she overheard the host introducing her.

"Fellas, fellas, fellas. Coming to grace the stage is the lovely, beautiful, big fine ass stallion, Rain. Hands down, she is one of, if not, the finest girl in here tonight. So fellas so come out them pockets and show my girl some love. And don't be cheap."

Just then, Rain slowly yet seductively walked to the stage. She signaled for the DJ to play what she called, her money-making anthem, Private Dancer by Tina Turner. That song put her in a zone like no other.

She walked to the front of the staged and started feeling up her breasts. She slid her right breast out of the top she was wearing and started to lick around her areola, followed by sucking her nipple.

"Dutch marks or dollars, American Express will do nicely thank you." While Tina continued to sing, Rain was being put in a trance. By now she was topless and wearing nothing but a red thong, her heels and her mysterious mask. Her body moved like a snake as she slow danced; giving her audience a hell of a show.

She got on her knees and stuck 2 fingers in and out of her cleaned shaved pussy and then stuck them in her mouth. Just then, $1s, $5s, and a shit load of $10s flooded the stage. The more money they throw at her, the more she put on. She was loving this attention she was getting so much. They money was pouring in like crazy. Making in rain was an understatement. This was one of her best nights. She collected her money and blew the crowd a kiss.

As she turned to walk away, she noticed a familiar face in the crowd. Her mouth flew open so wide, her tongue could have rolled out like a red carpet. "You got to be fucking kidding me! What the fuck is he doing here!", she said to herself. She only hoped that he didn't recognize her. Especially after the show she just put on.

After she counted her money, Shante' made well over $1,700. But that wasn't what was on her mind at the time. "I can't believe this shit." She mumbled to herself. What was he doing there, all cheesed up with a dancer on his lap? She wanted so bad to walk over there and check his ass, but she couldn't do that without blowing her own cover. She decided to let it go for now until she can find a way to get to the bottom of it.

CHAPTER 11:
NIGHTS LIGHT THIS....

"Umm, yeah right there. Suck that shit baby. Damn you sure got a fiyah mouth piece girl." Evan was on the verge of exploding his seeds in her mouth. He hasn't fucked her face in a while, so he didn't want to cum just yet. With that in mind, he helped her to her feet and laid her on her back. He gave her soft kisses on her lips, then moved down to her breasts, stomach and thighs. He wanted to make her remember what she'd been missing. He placed circles in her inner thighs with his tongue. That sent shock waves through her body.

"Ouhhhhh baby, this feels so good. Damn I miss you." After giving her thigh kisses, he slid his tongue down to her already wet pussy, giving it more wet kisses and licking and sucking on her swollen clit.

"AUGHHHH, Uphmm. She moaned while squeezing his ears and locking his head in place with her thighs. Now it was her who was on the verge of cumming.

"Come on baby, cum in my mouth. Let daddy taste it." Evan ordered. It didn't take long for her to do just that. After drinking her juices, he slid his hard dick slowly inside of her even wetter pussy, giving her slow and long strokes.

He had to admit, her pussy was so good. Just as he remembered. It's been a while since they've been intimate, and he missed that.

Although he loved his wife Pamela, things just weren't the same in their marriage. The spark and fire was long gone. Pamela was a good woman and waited on him hand and foot. He wasn't happy but he didn't want to leave his wife. Selfish but he couldn't bear to see another man with her if he'd ever left. She was his, forever.

"Baby don't stop. Gimme' all that good dick I been missin'. I swear he don't do it like you." She dug her nails deep in his back while he was pumping in and out of her. She wanted to leave her mark to let it be known that regardless of his status, he still belonged to her.

"I'm 'bout to cum. Augh." He exploded inside of her. After catching his break, he realized that he wasn't wearing any protection.

"Shit. Got damnit! I forgot to put on a damn condom. I don't need any more outside kids." He was upset at himself for not remembering to wear a condom. All he needed was for her to get pregnant again and all hell would break loose.

"Whatever, Evan. I'm not trying to get pregnant again either. Trust me. So, don't worry. Oh, and make sure you remember to send me some extra money. Our child is growing up fast and becoming very expensive. The money you send is good but it's barely covering all the stuff I gotta' get. Keep me happy like you promised."

"Don't worry, you will get your money. Just don't bug me about it. I gotta' go. Got work in a few hours." Evan went into the bathroom to whip up. Afterwards he started getting dressed so he can make it home to prepare from work.

She watched him as he left for work. She stood up and lift the mattress to retrieve that 3 hundred dollar bills she took out of his wallet when he went into the bathroom to drain his bladder and freshen up.

"Fuckin' right," she said to herself as she stuck the money in her purse. She was happy that he hadn't look in his wallet. He had so many 20 and a few 100-dollar bills, he probably wouldn't have missed it anyways.

She had to make sure she got whatever she could get when it came to Evan. The money he'd been sending her wasn't enough. She needed more but he was set in stone about giving her just enough. That pissed her off. So, every time they would hook up, she would steal some extra cash from his wallet or pockets.

She got up, took a shower and got dressed. She looked around the hotel room to make sure she didn't leave anything before she left. The placed the room key on the night stand and headed home.

****

It was the middle of the work week for Shante' and she was exhausted. Working at the night club after getting off from her first job was really taking its toll on her. But she needed the money.

Today she had gotten off a little early because of her appointment with her eye doctor. It was time for some new glasses because her prescription has changed and her old glasses were giving her a headache and sharp eye pains. Sometimes it would get so bad that she would lose vision in her right eye. She needed that new prescription as soon as possible.

After she was done seeing the doctor, she decided to stop by to visit her mother. Lately, she has been so worried about her. It all had to do with her father and her mother missing work.

She pulled up to her mother's house and saw that she was already on the porch with her favorite drinks, B&J wine coolers.

"Hey mama. How ya' doing today?" Shante' hugged her mother and gave her a kiss on the cheek.

"Hey my baby. I'm doin' alright. I could be better though. How was work?" Pamela asked.

"It was ok. I got off early 'cause I had a doctor's appointment for some new glasses. The old ones gave me headaches. Where my daddy at?"

"Chile', your guess is as good as mine. That's been the million-dollar question lately. I see him when he come home and get ready for work. Eat, shower and back out the door he goes. I get a hug and some of those lame ass forehead kisses and poof, he gone again. It doesn't even make sense to cook 'cause I end up eating alone."

Shante' could see the hurt in her mother's eyes. She was always such a strong, happy woman who's smile would light up a room. But lately, all she saw was when she looked at her mother was pain.

She thought about telling her mother about spotting her dad in the strip club with some random dancer all over him, but she was sure her mother was gonna' question about HER being there as well. So, she tossed that theory out of her head.

"I'm sorry mama. I don't like seeing you so down like this. I am sure he has a good explanation for being gone all the time. It's probably his job Ma'. Maybe he has picked up more hours at work. You think that could be it? I mean, it's a possibility," Shante' knew better. She just wanted to give her father the benefit of the doubt.

"Girl please. Your daddy cannot work over 20 hours 'cause of his disability checks he get every month. And he ain't trying to mess up that nice chunk of change. I doubt that's the reason. Maybe he got another woman'. Shit, ya' never know," Pamela took a sip of her drink.

"Stop it mama! You know daddy would never mess with no other woman. He loves you. You're a good woman and a great mother and wife. Why would he want another woman when he got a queen at home? He wouldn't do anything to mess up things at home."

"Even a good woman gets fucked over Shante'. You can be the best wife or woman in the world and a man still will break you down. Leave all his footprints on your heart and never feel an ounce of guilt. I love your father, but he is no better than any other lying, cheating man out here." Pamela started to get teary eyed. "Plus, I haven't been able to go back to work. My old job said they ain't hiring right now. And you know at my age it's harder to get a job. So along with your absent father, that's been on my mind too. Just seems like a load ya know? So much pressure."

"Aww mama. You want me to talk to daddy? Maybe he will open up to me."

"No. I can talk to your daddy myself Chile. You just make sure you help us plan this party for your sister. She is excited about her big day and she been bugging the hell outta' me about it. I will be ok baby. Don't worry about me. It's my job to worry about y'all. Whatever problems me and your daddy having has nothing to do with y'all. Ok? I will be just fine my baby. I've been through worst, trust me."

"Yes ma'am. Well, let me get ready to go pass by the mall. I love you mama. Everything will be ok. You are a strong black woman. I will call you later ok?" She gave her mother a kiss and was on her way.

****

Shante' pulled up to the mall parking lot. She had to buy a couple of outfits and some party supplies for her sister's big day coming up. Like her mother, she hated doing things at the last minute.

She stopped in Dillard's to find a fitted dress and some slacks with a blouse. She always had to have a back-up plan when it came to outfits. Once she finished there, she made her way to the party supply store to get some decorations, candles, table decorations and party hats. She was glad that she'd decided to come to the mall during the week. There was less traffic plus the mall wasn't as crowded as it was like on the weekend.

After 2 hours of shopping, she was done and ready to head home. She didn't have any plans on cooking. So, before she left the mall, she decided to go to the food court to grab some dinner 'cause was no way in hell she was touching that stove tonight after the long day she'd had. She was beyond tired. All she wanted to do was go home, run a nice, hot bubble bath, eat and watch Sanford and Son reruns. That was one of her favorite TV shows.

She decided between pizza or Chinese food. "Chinese food it is," she said to herself. While she stood in line waiting to order her food, this cute little boy bumped into her leg. He was adorable and had the cutest little dimples.

"Now what do you say when you accidently bump into somebody Jr?" the child's father said. "I'm sorry miss," the little boy said. "Aww it's ok little man, what's your name?" Shante' asked him. "My daddy said I can't talk to strangers." He turned and walked towards his daddy.

As soon as she turned around to see where the little guy was headed, her heart damn near skipped a heat. It was Benny. She hadn't seen him since he showed up at her house with flowers for prom night some years ago.

She had to give it to him, Benny was looking even better than he did during their high school days. She became weak in the knees and her stomach was fluttering from nervousness and he still gave her butterflies.

"Shante'?" he couldn't believe his eyes. The woman he'd always loved and never stopped loving stood right before him.

"Daddy, I gotta pee." Benny Jr. was holding himself and doing a little dance.

"Ok son, we gonna' go home in a minute," he told Benny Jr., without taking his eyes off her. "Hey Shante'. How you been? You look, damn, you look good girl. Just as beautiful as the last time I saw you."

"Hey Benny. How are you? Cute son." she said while she was looking around. She wondered if Jovita was close by. She didn't need her popping up from behind. She still didn't trust that low down bitch.

"Thanks. Yeah, he got my looks. Look Shante', I know it's been some years since we've last talked. But from the bottom of my heart, I am truly sorry that I hurt you. I can't take back what I did and I know I am the reason why your heart is so cold. I never meant to hurt you. I was just young and dumb at that time. I didn't realize what I had. If I can take it all back, I would. My son is the only good thing that came out of a very bad situation. Just know that I never stopped loving you, and I never will." Benny hoped his words would warm her heart. He really missed her.

"I forgave you a long time ago Benny. I have moved on. Yes, it hurt but what's done is done. I still never got over the pain and heartache you caused me though. And you are right. Your son is a very handsome little fella'. He's a blessing from a train wreck. Look, it was nice seeing you, but I really gotta' go. I'm good. Take care."

Benny then grabbed her arm before she walked away. "Wait, hear me out first. I love you Shante'. I know it's asking a lot, but I was hoping that we can still be friends, if that's ok with you. I'd rather have you as a friend than to not have you at all Shante'. I still want you to be a part of my life. Think about it. Here, take my number. I hope to God that you use it sometimes. See you around, beautiful. C'mon lil' man." He handed her a card with his information on it. He grabbed Benny Jr.'s hand and headed for the restroom.

Shante's didn't respond to that last statement. She just turned and walked away, without even ordering her food. She'd lost all train of thought the moment she laid eyes on Benny again. All her old feelings for him came rushing back to her.

Although she forgave him years ago, it still hurt. She put the card in her purse and headed home.

****

"Ring." Shante' haven't made it inside for a second before her phone started ringing off the hook. "Shit". She rushed to the phone but the caller hung up.

She sat down on the sofa and started taking off her shoes. She was tired and hungry. She decided she was going to just order a pizza. Seeing

Benny and his son at the mall was still heavy on her mind. She had to admit, Benny Jr. was a very handsome little boy. He had Benny dimples, but he had lighter skin, and neither Benny nor Jovita was light skinned. Still, he favored Benny a lot.

She called Dominoes and ordered a medium pepperoni pizza with extra cheese. She showered and twist her hair up for tomorrow. "What's on TV?" Just as she reached for the remote, her house phone started to ring again. "Lawd I can't even get comfortable for nothin' in the world." She was annoyed.

"Hello!" she answered sounding pissed off. "I see some things never change. Girl you still answer the phone with all that damn attitude," said the caller.

"And who the fuck might this be?" Shante' was curious.

"Shante', it's me."

"Me who? I don't know nobody named Me!" Shante' said to the caller.

"It's, (sigh), it's me, Darlene Shante'. Look, I just called to see how you was doing."

"Yes in fuckin' deed. I know you ain't calling me after the bullshit you and that hoe of a friend Jovita pulled some years ago. Bitch you must be stuck on stupid to call my house. Matter of fact, how did you even get my house number in the first place?"

"Look, I ran into your sister the other day and she mentioned she was having a party. I asked her about you and she gave me your number. I know me calling is the last thing you expected and I am the last person you wanna talk to or hear from right now, but I really miss our friendship and I am so sorry about the way things went down. Shante' I did not set that thing up at the hospital. I found out she was fuckin' with Benny after you broke up with him. She ended up telling me what happened when you got to the hospital and y'all had that fight or whatever."

Darlene continued. "The day she called and asked about you coming to see her, she mentioned that the baby daddy was there but never gave his name or nothing like that. Yeah, I saw the baby but it was the day before I called you. When I found out that Benny was the baby daddy, I was shocked and pissed all at the same time. I know you was gonna' think I set it up, but I honestly didn't know he was the daddy or fuckin' with her behind your back Shante'. I don't even rock with Jovita no more after that bullshit she pulled. And to be honest, Benny may wanna' hop, skip and jump to get a DNA test for that child 'cause he wasn't the only nigga she was fuckin' with at the time she got pregnant with Benny Jr. I know that much. She told me 'bout the niggas she was fuckin' with but she failed to mention anything about her dealings with Benny. So, you see, I didn't have shit to do with that Shante'. I wouldn't do no low-down shit like that. All I ask is for yo' forgiveness, even if you don't wanna' be my friend again. I can understand. Just hear me out though. I was clueless and in the dark just like you." Darlene poured her heart out, hoping that Shante' would not only believe, but forgive her as well.

"Damn Darlene. That's really a lot to take in. I mean that shit really fucked my head up for a long time. I knew that hoe was shady but I wouldn't have thought she would stab me in the back even though she been feeling Benny; even when we talked. But I appreciate your honesty and I accept your apology and all, but I'ma have to think this whole thing through 'cause after all that shit went down, I started having major trust issues."

"I truly do understand Shante'. I probably would have thought the same thing if the shoes were on the other foot." Darlene understood.

"But wait, girl what you mean he need a DNA test? I just ran into Benny and his son in the mall today, and that lil boy looks JUST like Benny. He got his dimples and everything, he just lighter them him. Plus, Benny signed the birth certificate from what I heard."

"I'm telling you Shante'. Jovita was out 'chea fucking everything with a dick and 2 nut sacks. Benny damn sure wasn't the only one. That's all I'm saying."

"Well that's between them girl. I'm so over Benny and Jovita asses. So, you coming to Gina party? You know it's going down!"

Shante' didn't want to admit it, but she secretly missed Darlene. She was happy that she called and explained her side of the story. She had been trying to do that for years.

"Yeah I'ma come thru and show some love to Gina. Girl I really miss hangin' out. Thank you for not hanging up in my face again and hearing me out this time. Jovita is no longer my friend. I can't hang 'round bitches with bad names. Her rep is all fucked up."

"She was a hoe then, and she gon' die being a trashy hoe. Well girl let me go. I'ma get your number off the caller ID and take down my cell number too. Keep in touch and I'ma see you tomorrow night at the party." Shante' gave Darlene her info and say her goodbyes. Just then her doorbell rang.

"Pizza, 'bout time." She looked out the peephole and saw that is was her best friend and brother from another mother, Danny. "Waddup bro! I thought yo' ass was the pizza man." She welcomed Danny in and gave him a big hug.

"Hey sis, what's up witcha? I was in the area and said let me go holla' at my big head ass sis right quick." Danny joked.

"Boy fuck you." Shante' laughed. "Picture who just called me? Darlene! Of all people. She gave me the run down about how all that bullshit went down at the hospital the day she called me to go see Jovita's baby. And I busted Benny ass there. She said she didn't have shit to do with it."

"Oh yeah? What else did she say? You know you still gotta' keep ya' eyes open dealin' with bitches these days sis. Maybe she was telling the truth, who knows. But still, why after all this time she contact you? That's what I wanna' know."

"She did try to reach out to me through-out the years but I wasn't hearing shit she had to say at the time D. I heard her out tonight but I still don't trust no bitch. But you right. I'ma keep an eye on her ass."

"Yeah, do that. Don't put nothing past no bitch. Besides that bullshit, you still working at that club? Man, you know I hate you working at that stankin' ass club. It smells just like beaucoup weenie water in that back room. Plus they be havin' some stupid ass niggas in there. I don't wanna' have to put none of them niggas to sleep behind my big sis ya heard me." He was still very protective of her; just as he was when they were little.

"Boy I can take care of myself. I go in, do my thang and be on my way home bro. I'm good." Shante' knew he hated her working there but she needed the money for school.

"Aiight. Well I'ma see ya at the party tomorrow. 'Bout to go holla' at this lil broad I been kickin' it with. Love ya sis." He stood up and gave Shante' a big hug and headed towards to the door. As soon as he opened the door, the pizza man was standing there. Just then Shante' cover her mouth, and Danny pulled out his pistol.

"Nigga, what the fuck you doin' over here?!" Danny demanded.

The guy smirked while holding the pizza. He saw Danny's gun, but he didn't budge. "That'll be $12.99, bitch!", was all that he said, while staring at Shante'. Danny grabbed his gat and started pistol whipping his rude ass. "Nah get the fuck from 'round here." The pizza man stumbled to his feet and walked off. He didn't even bother to collect the money.

"You alright sis?"

"Yeah D., I'm good. Just glad you was over here." Shante' was a bit shaken up but she was ok after a while. Danny decided to stay over for a couple of hours to make sure that asshole didn't show up at her place again.

****

Pamela was laying down in her room watching TV. It was almost 8pm and she knew at any minute, Evan will come walking through the door. She contemplated on whether she would bring up his changes lately. Knowing Evan, he would probably brush it off. She just needed some answers.

"Pamela," Evan yelled from the living room as he closed and locked the front door. "Yeah, I'm upstairs baby?", Pamela responded.

"Woman you didn't cook nothing for me to eat? You know I'm 'bout to go to work."

"Well dear, I wasn't sure if you was gon' come home or not. When I cook sometimes, I end up eating alone or it goes to waste baby."

"Fine, I'ma just stop and get something to eat before I go to work", he said while walking towards their bedroom.

Evan begin to undress so he could shower and change for work. Pamela couldn't help but to admire how fine and handsome her husband was, even though he was pushing 50. He still had it going on.

As soon as he took off his shirt, Pamela sat straight up in her bed. Just as she was about to say something, Evan closed the bathroom door and started the shower.

Tears escaped her eyes as she sat in bed hugging her knees. Her and Evan haven't had sex in almost 4 months. So, there was no way in hell that she'd left those long scratches on his back. She was so hurt and devastated. Her God given intuition was right all along. Evan had been cheating on her with another woman. Another woman was sexing her man. The thought of that alone made her have a mental breakdown and she couldn't stop the tears from falling down her face. She was hurt.

CHAPTER 12:
LOVE JUST AIN'T ENOUGH

Gina stepped out of the hot, steamy shower and dried herself off. Her husband, Jeremy, was finally off for the rest of the weekend and she wanted to plan something special for him.

While he was at the gym, she took the time to set the mood. She lit cherry scented candles and sprinkled rose pedals from the foyer, living room and down the hallway leading to their bedroom. She went to Victoria Secret and purchased a red matching bra and thong set and some body lotion. Red was Jeremy's favorite color.

She had some red wine, along with strawberries and green seedless grapes. Instead of turning on her favorite radio station, FM 98.5, she decided to make a slow jam CD because the radio commercials would ruin the mood.

It has been a few weeks since her and Jeremy had time for themselves. They didn't have any kids yet and they both worked during the day. He was also a personal training at the gym on Magazine St. He had a passion for working out so he decided to become a Trainor for extra income and for the pleasure of working out.

Gina didn't mind him taking on the extra job, especially in something that he loved doing so much. But on the other hand, it took away from so much of their time together. She even suggested that he use the spare room as a gym so he could train at home. But he was against it. He said you can't get the same effect as a regular gym. So, she stopped nagging him about it. She just wanted to spend more time with her husband.

She put on her lingerie and some vanilla body lotion. She placed her hair in a ponytail and applied light make up. She looked at herself in the mirror, admiring her beauty and sexy body.

She laid across her bed, listening to her mellow moods slow jam CD. She opened her laptop, she decided to log into her Myspace and scroll through Myspace until Jeremy got home.

After she logged into her account, she noticed that she had 5 friend requests and 3 new messages. Four of the five requests were from random guys with mutual friends. One request was from Tony. She hasn't seen him a while. "Damn!" Tony was looking GOOD these days. She quickly accepted his friend request so she can scan through his page. She didn't see any pictures of him with any women, so she assumed he was single. She saw that he also left her a message.

She clicked on the inbox icon to read his message. It read:

Hey, my old neighborhood friend. I was just browsing through Myspace ya' heard me and I came across ya' page. How you been? I see ya' still looking good girl. I hear you got married right after high school. Congrats to you and the Mr. How's the married life though? Me, well I'm still single, with no kids. Life is good on my end. I can't complain. Well I don't wanna' take up too much of your time. But hit me up sometimes or whenever you get a chance. Holla back."

T.

For some reason, his message gave her butterflies. She was a married woman and had no business feeling like this. True, but the lack of time and attention that Jeremy gave her maybe played a part in that. Tony was her old neighbor and childhood friend. She didn't see any harm in talking to him. After coming to terms with herself about his innocent message, she decided to respond back:

Hey Tony. How are you? I am doing fine. You are looking good yourself I see. Damn how tall are you now? You 'bout as tall as Shaq! As for the married life, it's great. I am happy. Well, it was nice of you to hit me up. Make sure you stay in touch. Oh, and before I forget, I am having a party tomorrow night at the hall in the East. So, if you are not busy, swing on by! It was nice talking to you. Don't be a stranger old friend. Later

G.

Sending him that message put a big smile on her face. She never really paid him any attention growing up. He was a handsome boy that grew into a handsome young man. She wondered what made him contact her after all these years? Whatever his reason, she was happy he did.

She looked at the clock on her nightstand to check the time. It was going on 9pm. "Where the hell are you Jeremy?", she asked herself. Just as she was about to get up to get a drink of wine, her Myspace messenger notification indicated that she had a new message.

She flopped back down on her king size bed and went straight to her inbox. Another message from Tony. She also saw this he was currently online. He hadn't waste any time responding back to her message:

"Hey pretty G. Glad to see you've read and responded to my message. And to answer your question, of course I'ma slide through your party. By the way, happy early birthday. What time does it start beautiful? Hit me back. I'ma be online for a few. Let's rap for a minute."

T.

Gina was tickled pink. Here she was, all cheesed up from reading Tony's messages, while dressed in sexy lingerie and waiting on her husband to come home and sex her crazy. She figured she would just entertain Tony until Jeremy got home. Something to do to pass time.

They sent messages back and forth for about 30 minutes. She sent him one more message before she called it a night:

Well, ok handsome T. It's time I call it a night. It was very nice talking to you. Hope you show up at my party tomorrow night. Don't forget, it starts at 7pm -until. You can bring some friends. Hope to see you there. XOXO

G.

After hitting send, she logged off her Myspace account and closed her laptop. She decided to give Jeremy a call to see what time he will be making it home.

She dialed his number and it rung 4 times before going straight to voicemail. The second time she tried him, someone picked up on the first ring but didn't say anything. All she could hear was a TV playing what sounded like a football game in the background. Then the line went dead. She tried his number one more time, only for it to ring 3 times and go straight to voicemail.

She thought that was strange but dismissed it. She laid down and continued to watch TV. She only hoped she didn't fall asleep while waiting on him. Especially with lit candles through-out the house.

****

"Just a sorry ass nigga, I swear." Tracy hated the fact that right after they fucked, he always rushed out the door to go home to his wife. His cell phone rang and Tracy decided to see who was blowing his phone up. Of course, it was his wife, as usually.

Tracy and Jeremy met at the gym where he worked part time. They worked out together and had good conversation.

Just then, Jeremy came out of the bathroom to see Tracy holding his phone. "What the fuck you doing with my damn phone Tracy? I told yo' ass about all this jealousy shit. Damn. You gon' make a nigga stop fucking with you behind that bullshit. For real. Pass me my clothes and shit so I can get the fuck outta' here."

"Nigga' don't be bookin' me in my damn house. Next time bring yo' damn phone in the bathroom with 'chu. That muthafucka' was ringing off the hook, drivin' the piss outta' me. And for your information, I didn't answer it. I just wanted to see who was blowin' ya fucking phone up. Quit with all that trippin' and shit. It's not that damn serious." Tracy spat at him.

"Aww Tracy, yo ass! You know exactly who that was calling me. Stop the games. Ima see you tomorrow or what?"

"I thought ya' wife had a party tomorrow night? What you ain't going?" Jeremy had mentioned it about 2 weeks ago.

"Damn, I almost forgot about that. Well, I guess I gotta' get a raincheck then. Come give me a kiss baby. I gotta' go."

"Can I come to the party? We can just make like we just gym friends or something. No biggie. I'ma be cool and I'm not gon' say shit. I promise."

"You out cho' fuckin' mind? You know damn well you can't come to my wife party. You must be smokin' dope or somethin' if you think yo' ass just gon' scroll up to the party and blow my shit up. Nah. I'ma see yo' ass after the party. Now goodnight Tracy."

Tracy leaned in for a kiss and got up to lock the door behind him.

After Jeremy was gone, Tracy took out the phone that was used to take a picture of Jeremy's wife phone number and name. After logging on to Myspace, Tracy searched for and found Jeremy's wife page. Gina page was public so that meant all her information was open to whomever visited her page. She had photos of her and Jeremy, looking like the happiest couple to walk the planet. Then there was the party information.

"Bingo! "Nigga you ain't gon be the only one going to the party." Tracy wanted to be there, invited or not.

****

"Baby, what's all this?" Jeremy made it home and walked into a living room full of half melted, lit candles and rose pedals everywhere. This only meant one thing: Gina wanted sex.

"Hey baby, welcome home. How was your work out?" Gina came downstairs in her sexy red panty set and gave him a big hug. "Damn baby, you smell like cologne mixed with sweat. Maybe you should have showered before coming home."

"Sorry baby. I went straight from work to the gym. You lookin' good and all, but baby daddy tired. I had 2 clients to train tonight. Plus I'm tired from the first job. I'm sorry. I will make it up to you some other time. I promise. You got everything ready for ya' big party tomorrow ha?"

"Got damn Jeremy! We haven't had sex in weeks! It's always the same fucking excuse, you tired! Maybe if you quit that fuckin' gym bullshit, you would have more time for ya damn wife!"

"SLAP!"

"Bitch, don't raise your fucking voice at me. Fuck wrong with 'chu? Now I told yo stupid ass I was tired, and that's that! You wanna' cobb a fuckin' attitude 'cause I didn't come home when you wanted me to. You lucky a nigga love you enough to come home to your bullshit in the first place. Getting' tired of all your complaining lately Gina and all that back talk. And blow out all these fucking candles and sweep these bullshit ass roses up. Yo' ass gon' fuck around and start a fire with all this bullshit. And turn that bonk ass music off. Sound like a funeral up in this bitch. Fuck. I told yo' ass I was tired but you gotta' keep going off at the mouth. That's why I don't be wanting to come in the muthafucka' when I do get off. Yo' smart ass mouth! Move!" Jeremy brushed pass Gina while she cried and held her face.

She wasn't the least bit surprised when he slapped her. By now, she was used to the verbal, emotional and physical abuse from Jeremy. Yet she still stayed.

"I'm sorry baby. I set up all of this so we can spend some time together. I know you love me baby but I just need more time and attention from you. We barely go out together anymore and the love making seems nonexistent these days since you started working at that gym. I'm not trying to bitch and complain. I didn't mean nothing by it. I just miss you that's all. I miss us." Gina cried.

"You can miss me with that bullshit, that's what the fuck you can miss. Oh, and happy birthday." He tossed a silver, rectangular jewelry box at her that he retrieved from his gym bag. "See, a nigga thought about your ungrateful ass. Now come clean this shit up so I can go to bed. And hurry up and turn that damn music off too."

Gina sighed without saying another word. She didn't want to get bat in the mouth again. So she did exactly as he said.

CHAPTER 13:
PILLS & A PROPOSAL

It was Saturday, the day of Gina's 21st birthday and her big party. Pamela, Joyce, Gina, Evan, Shante' and a few of Gina's friends and family members all got together to help decorate the hall for the party. They had about 3 hours before the party started and the wanted to make sure everything was perfect and in order. Most of the decorations were already in place. They were only doing small touch ups and making sure the DJ booth and the food areas were set up correctly. Gina wanted her night to be perfect.

"Baby when I tell ya', when Mark turn 21, his ass better just sang happy birthday and get the shit over with. This is too much work Chile." Pamela and Joyce shared a laugh. Pamela was tired from the lack of sleep. Her and Evan still haven't had the talk that she desperately needed to have with him. But today was about her baby girl Gina. She decided to confide in Joyce about it instead.

Witnessing Pamela eying Evan with a twisted look on her face, Joyce wanted to dig for information. "Girl, what's wrong with 'chu? Why you lookin' at that man like that?"

Pamela snapped out of her daggering stare at Evan and turned to answer Joyce. She whispered so no one would overhear their conversation.

"So, the other night, he had the nerve to bring his ass home, asking for dinner. I didn't cook a damn thing 'cause when I do cook, his ass don't ever come home. And when he does, he don't even eat the shit half the time. But that ain't even the worst part Joyce. He takes off his shirt to get in the shower, and he got 3 big, long ass scratches on his back!"

"Oh no, girl, Fa' true?!", Joyce played shocked but inside, she was hot! She hadn't had sexual intercourse with Evan in over 10 months. So, if it wasn't her marks, then who the hell was it that put those scratches there, she wondered. "Girl, what did you do? I just know you went upside his damn head. That's what the hell I would have done if he was my husband!" Joyce had plans on doing just that the minute she got Evan alone. She was furious. It's bad enough she had to share him with Pamela, but to share him with yet another woman? Oh, hell to the no. This was some bullshit and she needed to get to the bottom of it. Quickly.

"I did what I always do and have been doing for some months now girl, I just cried. Sometimes I don't know why I still stay with him. Maybe it's because he was my first love, my first everything. And he is the father of my kids. But I would be lying if I told you that lately everything has been hunky dory. We don't even have sex like we used to. I have to beg for it or if not, I'm the one that initiates it. That shit gets old. I remember a time when Evan couldn't keep his hands off me. I know we've gotten older, but I know ain't a damn thang wrong with me. My gut always told me that it was another woman, but I thought I was just being delusional and over thinking. Well them scratches on his back sealed the envelope. Evan is having an affair. I don't know Joyce. I mean, what would you do if it were you? Would you stay?"

"Hell no! Stay for fuckin' what? To keep getting ignored and cheated on? I'm sorry honey but there is no way in hell I would stay with his cheating, lying ass. It's bad enough he don't bring his ass home. And when he does come home, he got scratches on his back from another woman? Oh but no. You better than me. What would I do you asked, I would go out and enjoy my life. Girl your kids are GROWN! What you gotta' stay in a marriage for them for? It's time for you to do you. Let that other woman have his ass. Maybe it's for the best. All these good looking single men out here. You better do like that song that Ray Parker Jr. sang, "A Woman Needs Love." I'm just saying. Get out and see other people. Shit, he out here doing it and obviously not giving a fuck if he is coming home with his back all marked up. Now that's some disrespectful shit right there. And you keep letting that shit that he do slide. A man gon' only do what you allow him to. It's time you put your foot down girl. Kick his cheating ass to the curb and start living your life. Get to know other people. You always cooped up in that house all day. I know a lot of men that would love to mingle with you. Fuck Evan."

Joyce gave the worst advice that she could possibly give, hoping that Pamela would take her up on her offer to see other men. She wanted Pamela dumb ass to fall right into her trap so she can scoop up Evan for herself, finally. She wanted him and she would go to any lengths to make sure he is all hers. Besides, she was beyond sick of hearing Pamela bitch and complain about her marriage. It gave her a headache. She wanted Pamela's life and she would crisscross whoever she had to crisscross to get what she wanted.

Pamela was an example of a weak bitch. Too stupid to roll with the punches. Evan could do so much better.

"I don't know Joyce. I can't see myself with no other man but Evan. I love him so much. So, you think that me seeing another man, or men, would make me feel better and mask all my stress troubles at home? What if Evan found out! Girl he would kill me." Pamela wasn't going for Joyce's advice on stepping out on her husband. She was hoping for a different answer or some better advice from her friend.

"Well, stay if you choose to. But two can play the game that he is playing. Get out and get to know other people girl. Ain't no harm in that, right? Look, we can go to a hole in the wall after the party. Just to get you out the house for a while. Ok?"

"Ok. I guess it won't hurt to get a breath of fresh air." Pamela agreed. They continued to do the final touches on the decorations while talking some more about their plans after Gina party was over.

****

It was well after 10pm and Gina party was jumping. The place was filled with wall to wall people. The DJ was playing all the latest hits and even threw some throwback New Orleans bounce music in the mix. Gina was lookin' fly. She wore a fitted coral and gold fitted dress, to match her decorations. She was the life of her own party.

Even Darlene showed up. Shante' was happy to see her. Danny and Tony showed up also. Tony had a couple of friends with him. One of the guys caught Shante's eye. He was tall, muscular with tattoos and sexy as hell. "Damn, he can get it," she told herself. He must've have felt her eyes on him because at that very moment, they made eye contact. He winked at her and she quickly turned away and started rocking back and forth to the music.

Someone tapped Gina on her should while she was so busy on the dance floor. She turned around to see that it was Tony.

"Hey Tony! I'm so glad you came. How you doin'?" Gina damn near threw herself into Tony's arms. Since chatting with him on Myspace the night before, she couldn't get him off her mind.

"Hey Pretty G. You know I wasn't gon' miss your big day. Happy birthday beautiful. You look nice. Here you go." He pulled out 2 crispy hundred-dollar bills and pinned it on her birthday money pin.

"What's up playa, I'm her husband, Jeremy. I don't believe we've met." Seeing his wife hugged up with some dude almost sent Jeremy into a rage. He decided to introduce himself, seeing that Gina was too busy in love land to do so. He extended his hand to Tony for a hand shake.

"Oh, hey Wassup man. I heard all about you. Yeah me and Pretty G, I mean, Gina, yeah, we grew up together. We go way back. You're a lucky man. Nice to finally meet you though. I'll see you around Gina. And again, happy birthday." With that, he turned and joined the rest of the party.

"We'll be seeing your around," Jeremy spat, but Tony ignored his smart remark.

"Hey baby, wanna dance with me? C'mon, they playin' my song, Slow Motion. Come dance with me, please?" Gina knew that Jeremy was pissed off and she didn't want him to cause a scene. So, she dragged him on the dance floor to deter his attention from Tony.

"Yeah, aiight. It's your day. Anything for my baby."

They made it to the dance floor and started giving the crowd a show. Gina started bending over, grinding her ass on Jeremy while he held on to her waist. They were having a blast.

Shante' was bobbing her head to the music, until she noticed that her father was standing in the corner alone. This was the perfect time to finally get a chance to talk to her father. She knows her mother told her that she didn't want her getting involved in their marital problems, but she just couldn't stand to see her mother so down and out, knowing that her father was the reason. She made her way over to Evan to spark up a conversation.

"Hey daddy. Why you over here all by yourself? Where's mama?"

"She round here somewhere with that nosey bitch Joyce. How you been doin' my baby? How's school coming along? Did you enroll yet?"

"I'm doing good daddy and I enroll in a couple of months. I just been saving up ya know? But daddy, I been meaning to talk to you about something. Can I ask you a question? Just promise not to get angry and please don't mention anything to mama. But is everything ok at home?

I mean, lately mama has been seeming so down. She mentioned that sometimes you are never home, even on your off days. I just should ask. Is there another woman daddy? Mama sure seem to think so. I don't like to see the pain in her eyes every time she mentions you. I just want to know if everything is ok."

"What did we teach you about staying in a child's place? Whatever problem me and your mama having is between me and your mama, not you. Your mama knows how to come and talk to me when she wanna' know something. And as far as me seeing another woman, that's nonsense. You know how much I love and respect your mother Shante'. I just been a lil stressed out with work that's all. I miss being a Fire Chief. Ever since my injury, I just haven't been in my happy place ya know? But I swear, it has nothing to do with your mother, ok? Stop worrying so much. I swear you are your mothers' child." He gave her a hip bump then kissed her on her forehead.

"Ok daddy. Well let me finish enjoying the party. I love you daddy. Maybe you should surprise mama and take her out on a date or something. Get her some roses. Take her to the show. Anything. I just miss seeing that smile of hers."

"I'ma take your advice baby. Now go enjoy the party with ya' sister and daddy loves you too baby." Evan felt like cramp for lying to his daughter. He knows lately he haven't been a good husband to Pamela, but he wasn't happy at home. Yet, he couldn't bring himself to leave either. So, to make life easier for himself, he played the field. What Pamela didn't know won't hurt her. He never had any plans on leaving her, despite what he told Joyce. It's cheaper to keep her, he always told himself. But with Joyce in Pamela's ear and pretending to be her friend, he knew it was a matter of time before their secrets came to surface.

He hoped like hell that she wouldn't open her big ass mouth, or he would stand to lose a lot.

****

It was now 11:25pm, and the party would be over at midnight. The second line band was due to enter the hall at 11:45.

Mark was in the restroom, saying a silent prayer to himself. "Lord, I hope and pray that I am doing the right thing. Give me strength for what I am about to do. Amen." He got out of the stall, looked at himself in the mirror and let out a sigh. "Here goes nothing."

He walked pass the crowd on the dance floor and headed straight for the DJ booth. He tapped the DJ on his shoulder and asked to lower the music and to hand him the mic.

"Excuse me everybody, can I get y'all attention please. This only gon' take a minute." He headed towards the table where Pamela, Evan, Darlene, Shante' and Nadia were sitting, along with their baby girl Melody.

Everyone, including Nadia, stared at Mark, wondering why he stopped the party. He walked up to Nadia, and grabbed her hand.

"Baby, from the first time I saw you in the hallways at school, I knew I wanted to spend the rest of my life with you. You are the love of my life, my best friend and the mother of our beautiful baby girl Melody. I want to spend the rest of my life loving you and waking up to that beautiful face every morning. You have helped me grow from a boy into a man. You have always loved and been there for me, and for that, I love you. I just need this one thing from you." He got on one knee and pulled out a small box with a beautiful ring inside. "Nadia Thomas, would you do me the honor of being my wife?", Mark said with tears in his eyes.

To say Nadia was shocked was an understatement. She wasted no time answering Mark's question. "Yes baby, yes. Oh my God! I love you so much!" Nadia was overjoyed as Mark slide the ring on her finger. He picked her up and swung her around. Everyone was clapping and saying their congratulations. Some even shared a tear. Nadia wore the biggest smile on her face and she still couldn't believe he proposed to her. She walked around showing of that beautiful rock on her finger.

Just then, the DJ turned on the R&B bounce version of "He Proposed" by Kelly Price while Mark and Nadia made their way to the dance floor.

Everyone was excited, except for Evan. He thought his son was making the biggest mistake of his life by marrying so young. He wasn't even 21 yet and he hadn't finish enjoying his young life. He told himself that he would have a word with Mark about his decision. But tonight, was just not the time. He didn't want to ruin the moment for them.

Everyone was busy singing, dancing and congratulating Nadia and Mark on their engagement and having a good time. Outside, the second line band was getting ready to roll in and end the party with a bang.

Tracy picked the perfect time to get out the second line umbrella and Indian suit along with a Mardi Gras mask.

The band rolled in and the party went wild. "Do Whatcha' Wanna" blared through the speakers as everyone got on the dance floor and dance around Gina. Tracy danced up to the birthday girl, walking right pass Jeremy and got someone to take a picture of them. "Congrats on your birthday honey." Tracy had plans for Gina and Jeremy. Big plans.

****

"Until you come back to me, that's what I'm gonna' do." Joyce and Pamela went Uptown to a hole in the wall after Gina's party. They were sitting at the bar, jamming to the music.

"Girl this place is nice. Got a nice vibe to it. How often do you come here?" Pamela asked looking around. She told herself that she was happy that Joyce talked her into going out. She needed to escape her harsh reality pertaining to her marriage. Going out won't solve the problem but it sure gave her a breath of fresh air.

"Girl I come here all the time. The music good, the crowd is nice and the drinks, baby, if you wink at one of these fools, they gon' keep ya' stomach full of them drinks all night. Go mingle with all these fine, single and paid men in here girl. I'ma order our drinks. What you want?"

"You know I only drank wine coolers girl." Pamela said laughing. "Let me go run to the restroom right quick. Just give me a strawberry flavored wine cooler."

"Ok." She rolled her eyes and ordered their drinks. As soon as the bartender handed her the drinks, Joyce looked around the club to make sure Pamela wasn't coming and to make sure no one saw what she was about to do.

She pulled out 2 capsules of white powder, opened them and poured into Pamela's drink. She swished the bottle around to make sure the substance was well mixed in with the drink. "Oh yeah, I'ma make sure you have a good, good night." She smiled to herself as she saw Pamela coming from the restroom.

"Here you go girl. Drink up 'cause that damn drink was $5." Joyce smirked as she watches Pamela down here drink like she was dying of thirst. "Damn, this drink got an extra kick to it tonight girl."

"Yeah the club drinks tend to be a lil stronger. Let's go on the dance floor." Joyce led Pamela to the dance floor and they were having a ball.

She noticed that Pamela started flirting back with this one guy that's been hitting on her since they first stepped foot in the club. He made sure to hold her attention all night. Joyce got a sense that Pamela's drink was starting to kick in. Pamela and the guy left the dance floor and sat at a table in the back of the club.

At first Joyce lost sight of her because the club was getting crowded, but then she found Pamela sitting on the guy's lap who had her attention all night. "Gotcha." Joyce pulled out her camera from her purse and took a few pictures of Pamela and the random guy. They were making out like it's nobody's business. He even had his fingers up Pamela's skirt. By the way she was leaning her head back and moving her hips, she can tell that the guy was finger fucking her. Joyce was enjoying every minute of it.

"The minute Evan sees these pictures, he gonna' leave her gullible ass for good. This was easier than I thought. She 'bout a dumb bitch."

She saw the guy help Pamela in the next sit and she laid her head on the table. The substance that Joyce poured into her drink finally knocked her out cold. Pamela's date for the night walked up to Joyce and gave her a kiss on the cheek.

"All done Miss Lady. Man, you one cold-hearted woman. If that's ya' friend, then I would sure hate to be your enemy. Damn. My job here is done. Just gimme' what 'cha owe me so I can be on my way. I don't want no part of this bullshit when she wakes her ass up." She handed the guy 300 dollars. "Here you go, now get outta' here before she wakes up." He grabbed his money and placed it in his jeans pocket. "Goodnight", he said while heading for the entrance.

Joyce didn't want to be the one to do so, so she asked the bartender to call a cab for Pamela. "Hey, can you call my friend a White Fleet cab? Here is her address and the money to get her home." Joyce handed the bartender Pamela's address along with a 50-dollar bill.

"Why the hell you ain't taking her home? Didn't she come up in here with you?" The bartender was curious.

"That ain't none of ya fucking business. Now call her a damn cab. Here, take another 50 and shut the fuck up and focus on making them high ass drinks. That's all the hell you need to worry about." She rolled her eyes and tossed him another 50.

"Shiddd, aiight!" He was happy to get that 50-dollar tip and called the cab for Pamela. By the time the cab arrived to take Pamela home, Joyce was already long gone.

CHAPTER 14:
DADDY'S MAYBE

"Wassup Pops. What 'chu up to?" Mark went to visit his daddy after he called and said he wanted to speak with him about something very important.

"I'm good son. How's my grandbaby? That girl knows she is growing up fast." Evan asked.

"You right about that. She is getting out of the way quick. Me and Nadia thinking about giving her a lil brother soon. After we married and all. I'm so excited 'bout that. So glad she said yeah. I was nervous as a hooker in church when I asked her to marry me."

"Son, that's what I been meaning to talk to you about. Look, I know you love Nadia and I know she loves you too. She is your first love and the mother of my precious grandbaby. But why are you so in a hurry to get married? I mean, don't get me wrong, she is a lovely girl and all, but why the rush? You are still young. You haven't even lived out your young life yet. You 'bout to give up your freedom and not to mention, pass up on all of this good pussy out here. Ya' know what's gon' happen. You gon fuck around and marry that woman, and she gon' start having baby after baby and then she gon' start gaining all that weight. Then you gonna' feel trapped. That's when the cheating and creeping and shit gon' start." Evan was feeding his son the ugly truth. At least that's what he thought. "All I'm saying is, just give it some thought son. Hold off on the date of the wedding for about another 2 or 3 years before you go jumpin' the broom."

"Oh, so you want me to be like you? Like how you stay out all night on my mama? Like that? Look, I'm happy, she happy. WE happy! So, if you not gonna' be happy for me pops, then you can ride out! Straight up. I ain't livin' for you or nobody else." Mark was furious.

"What goes on with me and ya mama ain't none of your damn concern. First ya' sister and now you comin' at me with this bullshit about my fucking marriage. My business is my business. Look, I support you son. I just wanted to talk some sense into you before you make that big ass leap. I'ma be there for you son. Just voicing my opinion."

"Good, 'cause that's all it is, an opinion. Where mama at? I mean you no disrespect Da, but this conversation is over." By then, Mark was done talking to his father. He knew all about his dad's late nights in the strip club. A couple of his homeboys spotted his daddy in there, throwing cash at strippers left and right. They ran it by Mark and he said he would deal with it. He never mentioned it to his father or anyone. He wanted to catch his father in the act for himself.

"She down by Joyce house. I'll tell her you stopped by."

"Cool. I'ma holla'." Mark made his was to his car without so much as a hug or a hand shake to his father and drove off.

****

Benny decided to have a father-son day at the park Uptown. He'd been so busy working that he hasn't been spending a lot of time with his son.

It was after 3pm and the park wasn't as crowed as it usually is. There were a few kids playing on the playground and some was shooting basketball. They even had a few nice looking young ladies there with their kids. Alone.

Benny Jr. was playing on the sliding board with another little kid. Benny decided to walk over and assist Jr. on the toys. "Wassup lil fella'." Benny spoke to the other little boy that was playing with Jr. "Hey Mr.," was all the little boy said.

"Be careful honey. Take your time." Benny turned to see a beautiful, curvy woman, assuming she was the child's mother, coming towards the little boy. "Ok mama."

"Hello Miss Lady. This lil fella' here is your son? He gon' be a lil' heartbreaker like my boy. His name is Benny Jr. I'm Benny. Nice to meet you beautiful." Benny couldn't help but to flirt with the attractive young woman. She was short with hazel eyes, curly light brown hair with beautiful brown skin.

"Samantha, most people call me Sam though. Nice to meet you Benny. And yes, he's my little guy. We come here often. It's his favorite place to play besides Chuck E. Cheese. First time seeing you guys here though. Do you live in the area?" She questioned Benny. She couldn't help but to notice how sexy he was. She knew he was checking her out as well. So, she flirted back.

"I'm from Uptown. I just work so much and I don't get to take Jr. to the park a lot ya' know? Had to clear my schedule today and take lil man out to spend a day with him. So, are you from around here? You got a man, husband, etc.?"

"No, I'm from Kenner but my people stay Uptown. I be chilling by them sometimes 'cause Kenner is so boring. My friend was supposed to meet us up here but I guess she is running late, as usual. I'm not gon' be out here too long though 'cause I gotta' go home and cook in a lil' bit. And to answer your question, I'm very much single. No man and I damn sure don't have a husband. How about you? Handsome as you are I know somebody lockin' you down." She flirted with Benny.

"No ma'am. I'm single. I just work, go home and spend time with my lil one. That's about it. But look, since you say you single, can I be ya' lil friend? We can chill, go have a drink or somethin'. No harm in just chillin'."

"What the fuck?! I know you ain't out chea' with my son, picking up hoes!" Jovita came storming across the park with one hand on her hip. She noticed Benny playing Mack daddy with some chick in front of their son.

"Jovita what the hell is wrong with you and what 'chu doing here anyway? It's my time to chill with lil man. Take yo' ass home somewhere. You always startin' some shit."

"Boy don't tell me what the fuck to do. I told you have him back by 3:30 'cause we going to a party. And you out 'chea spittin' yo' weak ass game to this hoe."

"Who you callin' a hoe? Bitch you lucky them kids out there or I'll slap the stupid off ya face. You don't know me to be calling me out my name. Benny, it was nice chattin' with 'cha but I see you got your hands full with that one. Come on son, let's go." Samantha called for her son and they headed towards her car to leave.

"See that's what the fuck I be talking about. I can't spend one day with my son without you cutting into my time with this bullshit. I pay my child support on time and get lil man whatever he needs. But no, I can't even have my time with him in peace 'cause yo' ignorant, salty ass always gotta' come and fuck it up. And you can't tell me who the hell I can and can't have around my son. All them niggas you be laid up with, girl please. And it's just 3 o'clock! I still got 30 minutes before I drop him off back to you. What you can't tell time or somethin'?"

"Nigga I don't have no niggas around him. And if I do that's my business. Don't be trying to use my son to pick up them stank ass hoes you be flirting with. With yo' weak ass game." Jovita said with her neck rolling.

"I see my weak ass game got you! Couldn't be that damn weak 'cause I ran up in that high mileage ass pussy."

Jovita hauled off and slapped fire from Benny's face. "I told you 'bout playing with me." Jovita wasn't having it. Right in the middle of the park, she started whaling on Benny, failing to land a single blow besides the first one.

"Stop it Jovita! Jr. right there. Why you gotta' be so fuckin' difficult bruh. You ain't gon keep puttin' ya fuckin' hands on me either!"

"Thump!" Both Jovita and Benny turned to witness Benny Jr. laying face first on the ground, covered in blood and he wasn't moving.

NOOOOOO! Jovita ran to her son and lift him up and started shaking him. "Wake up baby, GET UP! Benny call the ambulance. My baby not moving! Oh Lord no, please. HURRY UP BENNY!"

"Come on, I'ma take him to Charity. Let's go. He is bleeding out a lot. He is losing too much blood. We ain't got time for no ambulance." Benny picked Jr. up and ran to the car. Jovita helped place Jr in the back seat and she also sat in the back, holding his hand. "Baby get up, please wake up my baby. I'm so sorry." Jovita cried over Jr, praying that he will be ok.

****

"Gotta' make sure I got everything." Shante' was getting her backpack ready for the bachelor party her and Fancee agreed to do for Jon Boy. She was nervous, just like right before she went on stage, but she felt a little at ease knowing that she will have someone there dancing with her.

Bunny called her earlier with the details of the party. The cost of doing the party was $2,400, split evenly between herself and Fancee. Plus tips. She desperately needed the money so she had to prepare to work harder for those tips.

After double checking her bag and looking at herself in the mirror, she headed for the front door to leave. Just as she opened the door, her house phone rang. She looked at the caller ID to see that it was Darlene.

"I'ma just call her back when I get back home." She let it go straight to voicemail and was out of the door.

****

Fancee was already parked outside of the location of the bachelor party. She was in the car, chilling and rollin' a blunt. She always got high and took a couple of shots before her performance. It soothed her and made her body have a mind of its own while she danced.

Her cellphone rang before she could light up her blunt. "Hey what's up? Yeah. I'm here, waiting on her now. Look, you can't call me while I'm in there 'cause I'm not gon' have my phone on me."

"But look, I'ma ask her can she work for me this Saturday night, and if she says yeah, I'ma set everything up. I don't want nothin' leading back to me. So, once you do what you gotta' do, get the fuck. Don't leave no traces 'cause if you get caught, that's all on you. Ok?"

The caller on the other end agreed. "Ok, yeah, love you too. I gotta' go now. She just pulled up." Fancee ended her call and headed towards Shante's car.

"Hey boo, you ready to make this mullah? I can tell by these nice ass cars parked out here that these niggas in here bankin'."

"Yes girl, shit give me a pull of that blunt 'cause I'ma need it. This my first time doing a private party. I just hope these niggas ain't assholes." Shante' was ready to get it over with already.

"Girl just focus on that paper. Let's get in here." Fancee led the way.

****

"Shake ya ass, watch 'cha self." Fancee and Rain was giving it all they got! They were making their asses bounce, shake and clap to the beat and the fellas were in ass heaven.

Shante', stage name Rain, had over 5 shots of that dark liquor and it was taking its effects on her. She even gave Jon Boy a lap dance, topless in a thong, and of course, her mystery mask for the night.

Fancee was used to these types of private parties. She did over 50 of them in her stripper career. She couldn't help but to notice how Rain was so comfortable around the fellas. She was shocked. She wanted to turn it up a notch. She needed to take her out of her comfort zone.

She walked over to the radio and put in her R&B cd. The song, 12-Play, by R. Kelly roared through the speakers. She motioned for the fellas to have a seat and walked over to Rain and grabbed her by the hand.

She led her over to where Jon Boy was sitting. It was his night and his last night as a single man. She wanted to make it worth his wild. She whispered instructions to Rain and she followed suit.

First she slow danced with Rain' to lightened the mood. Even after having many drinks, she still sensed her nervousness. "Just follow my lead baby girl. You gon' be alright. Trust me." Fancee promised.

As the song played on, Fancee and Rain were dancing and feeling each other up. They even took it a step closer and started tongue kissing. Fancee stuck her index finger in Rain's pussy and let her taste her own juices.

"Shit, bring that shit over here!" Jon Boy said while rubbing his dick, and licking his lips. "Come here." He signaled for them both to tend to his needs. "I wanna' know how that pussy taste", he told Fancee.

"You gots that." She guided Rain to the floor. Once down, she slid her thongs off and threw them to the side. She removed her top and thongs off and placed them on the side as well. She stood in between Rain's legs and Jon Boy's chair, and got in the hand-stand position. Once there, she placed her face in Rain's pussy and her pussy in Jon Boy's face. They wasted no time being sucked on and tasting on each other.

"Oh shit!" The fellas in the room started throwing cash while "Ohhing & Auhing" at the performance the girls were giving, wishing it was them getting pleasured. Rain was moaning heavy while Fancee was devouring her pussy. And Jon Boy was eating Fancee from the back. He even stuck in his tongue in and out of her asshole. This made her hot! She wanted to take it a step further. Without coming up from Rain's pussy, she grabbed the zipper of Jon Boy's pants and pulled out his dick. She reached down lower and started to massage his balls. "Shit." It's my fucking party, and you got a tasty pussy, but now I wanna know what that mouth do. Come taste this dick. Both of y'all."

Fancee and Rain both got on their knees and took turns slobbering up and down Jon Boys' shaft. They would rotate from his dick and back to his balls.

"Fuck this shit. Let's take it to the back." Jon Boy ordered.
Within minutes, they were headed to the back room to finish their 3some in private.

"Get yo big fine ass on this bed. Ass up!" Rain did as he said and climbed on the bed on all fours while Fancee positioned herself behind Jon Boy. Out of nowhere, Fancee pulled out a brown colored dildo. She wanted to do some extra freaky shit, but he wasn't having it.

"Bitch is you crazy? You must be out 'cho rabbit ass mind. Oh fuck no. Da fuck you think you 'bout to do with that big ass rubber dick? Ain't no muthafucka getting behind or in my ass. I ain't with that fun boy shit y'all be doin' at the club. That's dead. Go sit yo' ass on her face. You gon' have yo' time to hit this head right after I dig out this pussy."

Fancee crawled on this bed and positioned herself over Rain's face. She kind of sensed that Rain was nervous and had never down this before, so she put her at ease.

"Just do it like I did yours. It's gon' come easy to you. Just lick me where I licked you." Fancee gave play by play instructions. Rain loosened up a little bit. She had dick in her pussy and pussy in her mouth. She'd never done this before, but she was learning to love it. This was her first threesome and first experience being with a woman, let alone eating another woman's pussy.

After sucking and fucking on each other for 5 minutes, Fancee slid down on top of Rain and started tongue kissing her. Jon Boy stepped back and started pleasuring himself while watching the scene before him.

Fancee started fingering Rain, going in and out of her wet pussy using 3 fingers, and at the same time, tasting her juices. Afterwards, she started to tongue kiss her, while grinding her pussy into Rain's pussy. They both let out moans. Rain has never experienced this type of pleasure before. She came almost instantly. Fancee came shortly after.

Jon Boy had seen enough and wanted to join in. "My turn. Keep that shit going." While still laying on top of Rain, Jon Boy stuck his dick in between their two pussies. He went from doing that to taking turns sticking his dick in Rain and back in Fancee.

"I'm 'bout to nut. Come catch this shit." Both ladies turned around with their mouths wide open to catch his cum. They didn't let one drop hit the bed. After they were done, Jon went into his jeans pocket and pulled out 2 wads of money.

"Here you go ladies. Thanks for a good night. Y'all can go in back bathroom up the hall and clean up while I lock up behind my boys."

"See girl, I told you them niggas was bankin'. You enjoyed yourself?"

"Yeah, it wasn't that bad. Even though you know I never did no shit like that. I was a lil' nervous at first. I guess that powerful as blunt you gave me plus them shots helped me relax."

"Shit, this over $2,000 girl! That nigga broke bread tonight. I know that broad he is marrying know she hit the jack pot with that nigga." Fancee counted her money and put it in her bag.

"You gon' be alright to drive home?" She wanted to make Shante' got home safe.

"Yeah I'm good. I gotta got put this shit in the bank Monday morning girl. Thanks for helping me loosen up tonight."

Fancee walked Shante' to her car, gave her a hug and was on her way home. Shante' got in her car and checked her phone to see she had over 10 missed called from Darlene. "Damn why is she blowing my shit up like that?" she wondered. Just then she heard a knock on her driver side window.

"Hey, you need something?" She asked without rolling down here window. "I just wanted to holla at 'cha. That's all. I don't bite. I was at the bachelor party tonight. I thought you were beautiful."

She opened her door to step out and talk to the gentleman. "Hey, I'm Rain, well Shante'. How are you?"

"I'm Chad, and man, you sexy as hell. You did a good job tonight. You seemed a lil' nervous though. That's your first time doing a private party?"

"Yeah, I never done a private party before. I only worked at the club for a year because I am saving to put myself through school. I don't do it for pleasure, trust me. I have a day job too. Just trying to save up. You know how that is. I must say, my girl caught me off guard with that stunt she pulled. I'm still a lil shocked."

"Yeah, I peeped that. My nigga Jon Boy known for having them wild ass parties though. So, I wasn't a least bit surprised. But hey, I ain't here to judge. I just wanna get to know you as a person, not the dancer." Chad was intrigued by Shante's beauty.

"I mean, it seemed a lil strange cause you just saw me busting it wide open and shit." The both shared as laughed.

"Baby girl, it's a job. You have a purpose. I get it. I know some chicks that been in the game for years with no goals or plans on getting out. I know college is a muthafucka to pay for. Once you get that degree, it's gon' be all worth it. You ever thought about stopping though? I mean, they got some crazy ass niggas out 'chea. I'm just saying. Make that money, true, but you gotta' be careful."

"I know. And trust and believe my ass don't plan on dancing forever. Like you said, I have a purpose. Well It's getting late and I am high and tired. Take my number and hit me up sometimes. Maybe we can go on a real date. You get to see me with my clothes on." She giggled and wrote down her number.

"Cool black. Put this number in your phone. Let me know when you are free so we can hang out. Stay beautiful." He winked at her and they both went their separate ways.

Danny and his date were enjoying their dinner date at Olive Garden.

****

"So, when we gon hook up again? You know yo' ass hard to catch up to. Probably be with ya other hoes." Danny's date said jokingly.

"Stop playin' with me. Man, you know a nigga be out 'chea grinding. I chase dollars, not hoes. And why every time we chill you gotta' bring up other chicks? Like chill on that shit."

Just then his cell phone rang. "Hold on baby I gotta get this."

He stood up and walked towards the restroom to talk in private.

"Hello? Wait…slow down. What happened? Aiight, aiight. I'm on my way. Damn." Danny hung up and headed to his date to deliver the bad news.

"Look baby, take this money for the food and call a cab home. I gotta' make a quick stop but I'ma get up with 'cha later." He dashed out of the door and headed to the hospital.

****

"Doc, what do you mean my blood is not a match? This is my son!" Benny was lost, scared and confused. Benny Jr. had lost a lot of blood and needed a blood transfusion immediately. Benny decided to be the blood donor for his son, but his blood type wasn't a match.

"Calm down Mr. Wilson, your blood and you son's blood is not a match. It's impossible for you to give blood. Although his mother is a match, she cannot donate blood to your son for health reasons.

"Why not? That's his mama! My baby in there bleeding out and you telling me neither me nor his mama can save him? Why can't she give him blood?!"

"I'm sorry Mr. Wilson. But I'm not at liberty to discuss that with you. For confidential reasons. Excuse me." The doctor left the waiting room.

"Man, FUCK bruh!" By now, Benny was punching the wall, causing a scene.

"Sir, if you don't calm down, we are going to have to get security in here to escort you out of the hospital. Now I am sorry about your son, but I think it's best if you cool off and have a talk with the child's mother. She knows more than she is saying about the identity of that child's biological father." The nurse informed and stepped out of the waiting area to check on Benny Jr.

Jovita sat across the waiting room, watching Benny walk back and forth. She was so worried that her son wouldn't make it, but she was terrified to find out that Benny finally knew that he wasn't Jr's biological. She didn't think he would ever find out, especially not this way.

They sat in quiet for about 20 minutes until a familiar face walked in. "Jovita, where's my son?

"Your son? Nigga what 'chu mean your son?" Benny was heated. He stood face to face with the man claiming to be Benny Jr.'s real father.

"Nigga you ain't the only nigga with dimples. You ever wondered why Benny Jr. was so light skinned? Lil man look like he can be either one of our son. So, don't come at me my nigga. You need to bring all that negative energy to the bitch who you laid up with. Just like she lied to you, she lied to me too."

He then turned to Jovita. "So Jovita, you gon' tell him the real? Ain't no sense in sitting over there looking stupid now. You gon' tell this man how you told me you were pregnant and I gave you the money for the abortion and ya' grimy ass kept the baby and the money, and pinned the baby on this man? Man, I found out 'bout 2 years ago this lil man was mine. She been having me coming around acting like I was his uncle and shit. Knowing that lil man my is fucking son. I couldn't tell lil man that I was his real daddy. You the only daddy he know man and I didn't want to confuse him. I been sending her money and everything for him bruh. Tell that man Jovita. Ain't no sense in crying now. Where my son at man?"

"He's in the operating room, Danny. He needs your blood and he need it right now. All that other stuff ain't even caused for right now D. Just please go help my baby, please." Jovita said with her head hanging low.

CHAPTER 15:
HALF-TRUTH

Shante' was at home, relaxing and chatting with Nadia about her and Marks upcoming engagement party at her grandmother's house. After doing the bachelor party the night before, Shante' decided to call in sick. She had a mild headache from both the weed and back to back shots she took last night.

"Girl y'all came up with a date for the wedding yet? I still can't believe my lil brother proposed to you. Girl you must really got his ass sprung and whipped. But on a serious note, I am so happy for y'all. I wish one day that it could be me getting married. Maybe one day." Shante' thought back to her and Benny.

"Don't trip Shante'. You will find love. Speaking of love, you know I seen Benny the other day ha? I think he still single girl. And he is looking damn good these days." Nadia threw hints but Shante' wasn't catching it.

"Chile please. I ain't trying to be no damn step mama. Especially dealing with Jovita. I saw him at the mall with his son Benny Jr. the day before Gina's 21st birthday party. I can't even lie, lil man was so handsome. Just like his daddy. To be honest with you, seeing Benny that day really bought back some old feelings. I forgave him but it still hurts the way he betrayed me. We probably would have been married with our own kids by now. Oh well. The past is the past. Besides, I met a new lil' friend the other night."

"Do tell! So when will we get to meet this "new lil friend" you speak of?" Nadia wanted to be nosey.

"Dang, I barely know him my damn self. I met him at this party. Still gotta' get to know him before I can bring him around. So back to this wedding. Y'all decided on a big wedding? Vegas? Small wedding? Will there be a wedding?"

"Yeah girl. Of course, there will be a wedding. We are thinking of doing it in 6 months. Just something small ya know? My grandmother will fill in for my mother since I never met her. Sometimes I sit and wonder what she is, or was, like. Whenever I ask my grandmother about my mother, she quickly changes the subject. But Ms. Pamela has been like a mother to me and you and Gina always treated me like sisters. So, I am thankful for the people that I have around. And your brother, such an amazing man and father. I wouldn't wanna' marry anybody else. Unless it's Denzel!" Both Nadia and Shante' gave each other hi fives while laughing. Just then the doorbell rang.

"Hold up. Who is it?" Shante' asked looking through the peep hole. It was Darlene. She opened the door. "Well damn girl, why yo' ass never answered your phone? I guess you haven't heard ha?" Darlene couldn't wait to fill Shante' in on what's been going on.

"Well, sis, let me go. I gotta' pick up Melody from by my grandmother's house. I'ma see y'all later. Nice seeing you Darlene. I'm glad to see that y'all are back to being friends again." She gave hugs to both ladies and was headed to her destination.

"So, what's up girl? I saw how yo' ass been blowing my phone up. What's the matter? Everything alright with 'chu?"

"Baby, you ain't gon' believe this shit what I'm 'bout to tell you girl. So, the other day, Benny was at the park with Jr. talking to some chick. Picture Jovita walked up on him and they got into a heated altercation in front the baby. While they saw so busy fussing back and forth, they weren't even paying attention to lil man. Next thing you know, he fell from the top of the monkey bars, face first. He was bleeding like crazy." Darlene continued to give Shante' the run down on what happened to Benny Jr.

"Oh no! Are you serious? Is he ok?" Shante' asked.

"Wait, but that ain't even the tripped-out part yet. So, they get to the hospital and was told that Benny Jr. needed a blood transfusion. Of course, his daddy volunteered but when they doctor ran tests, they said he is not a match for his son and they do not share the same blood type what so ever. And for some reason Jovita can't give him blood. Something about she got new tattoos or some shit like that. Girl, tripped my head all the way out. But you ready for the killer part?"

"Yeah bitch what? Spit it out!" Shante' was anxious.

"Guess who the daddy is? Danny!"

"Please tell me you are bullshitting Darlene. Did I hear you right? Danny? Like, my lil play brother, best friend Danny? Are you serious Darlene?" Shante' heard her but it still didn't quite register hearing that Danny is Benny Jr's biological father.

"Serious as cancer. Danny is the daddy. I heard it from the horse's mouth. Jovita ended up calling me and she told me everything that I am telling you. That dirty hoe knew Benny wasn't the daddy. Even though they did fuck around. Then she ended up finally telling Danny a few years ago 'cause her and Benny was supposed to get a DNA test. Something to do with the increase of his child support and Benny was against it. They just verbally agreed that Benny Jr. was Benny's son. They didn't sign no type of paper work nor was a DNA test needed since they both agreed. So poor Benny just took her word for it. Girl I would have to get the rest of the story from her cause a lot of shit ain't adding up. But what I think was, she really wanted Benny to be the daddy 'cause he was going places. But he ended up settling for a job working at a plant once he got word that she was pregnant. That hoe thought she was 'bout to hit a lick having his baby 'cause he played ball. Oops. Now that hoe looking dumb."

"Wow girl. This is just too much. I still can't believe that Benny is not that child's father. And Danny is? I didn't even know they had a thing going on. Let me call Danny right quick." Shante' went for her cell phone and dialed Danny's number.

"Hello. Hey sis. Look, I can't talk right now man. Some shit went down. I'm at the hospital. I'ma hit 'cha back." Danny hung up without giving Shante' a chance to respond or get a word in.

"Girl he said he is still at the hospital. I guess when he ready, he will let me know. And poor Benny. I know he is hurting behind this. Even though he regrets fucking with Jovita, he still loved that little boy. And wait, what about his name? That dumb bitch named that child after Benny, knowing that wasn't his son? Wow!" Shante' wasn't surprised. Jovita been low down.

"Girl, well. I don't know how that's gon' play out now Shante'. That poor child is gonna' be lost. Good thing Danny was a perfect match. The way Jovita was telling me, he was near death without that blood transfusion. I'm just glad lil man alright ya know?"

"Yeah, me too." Shante' agreed. She wondered how Benny was doing. She thought about calling him once Darlene left. Yes, Benny broke her heart and betrayed her, but no one deserved what he was going through right now. She went to her room to get her purse. She still had the card that Benny gave her at the mall.

"I think I'ma give Benny a call later girl. When I ran into him at the mall, he gave me his number, but I never called. He needs all the support he can get right now. I can put the past aside for now. Jovita is a sad ass chick. I feel so bad for Benny and his, well, Danny's son."

Darlene agreed. "Yeah, call and check on him. I am sure he will be happy to have your support." Darlene and Shante' talked for a little while before Darlene left.

****

Joyce was at home, washing the dishes and listening to the radio. She had been thinking a lot about talking to her son about the identity of his biological father. She figured she had all she needed to take the next step in her plan to win Evan.

"Hey ma'. Where you at?" Tony came into the house looking for Joyce. "I'm in the kitchen my baby?"

Tony walked over to his mother and gave her a kiss. "What you cooking ma? I'm hungry."

"Not a damn thang. You don't live here no more so I don't have no more reasons to cook Chile. And how you been doing son?"

"I'm good ma'. Livin'. You know how that is. Been chit-chattin' with a lil friend. That's about it."

"Oh yeah. So, who is this girl that got your nose all wide open?"

"You will meet her mama."

"Son, I been meaning to talk to you about something. But before I start, can you run me by the post office right quick? I gotta' mail off this letter. We can talk about it in the car. I gotta send this off before the post office close."

"Aiight ma'. Let me use the bathroom right quick."

While Tony was in the bathroom, Joyce went into her bedroom closet and placed the postal service box on her bed. She decided to only send the letter, not the whole package. She wanted to deliver that herself.

"You ready ma?" Tony yelled from the living room. "Yeah, here I come". They were headed to the post office.

****

After they came from the post office, Joyce decided she would take her son out to eat. They decided on Chilli's on Veterans. Besides, she wasn't in the mood to cook a damn thing.

They both ordered their food and drinks.

"Well son, here's the thing. I know I haven't been mother of the year, but you know I have tried my best to take care of you as much as I know how. I must say, although I cannot show you how to be a man, you turned out to be a bright young man."

"Aww, thanks ma. But where all this coming from?" Tony grew curious. His mother was talking in circles.

"Son, it's about your father. Your biological father. I have been in contact with him. It's time that you finally get a chance to meet him for yourself."

After that statement, Tony looked up from his plate and stared at his mother. "My father, but I thought he was de...."

"Dead? No son, he wasn't dead. He was more like a dead beat. The thing is, when I got pregnant with you, your father already had a family that I didn't know about. He would send me money for you every month and call to check on you, but during the time of you growing up, he couldn't physically be there for you. I didn't know about his other family. I didn't want to hurt you so I decided I just won't mention your father to you, until you were old enough to understand son."

To her surprise, Tony was ok with it.

"Well ma, I went all this time without him, so I really don't care to meet him now. Yes, you did a good job with raising me, and I love you for that. You've been mama and daddy all of my years growing up. So, no, I really don't want to meet him now, and never."

Joyce didn't know how to respond. She knew once that letter reached its destination, that everything will change. So what, she bent the truth a little bit. She just didn't want to look like the bad guy when the truth finally came out. She knew good and well that Evan was married before Tony was born. They ate in silence for the remainder or the time they were in Chilli's.

CHAPTER 16:
SPEAK THE TRUTH, SHAME THE DEVIL.

Danny, Jovita and Benny was sitting in the waiting room waiting to hear the results of Benny Jr.'s surgery. It's been a long day and everyone was restless.

When Benny got up to get some coffee, Danny decided to pull him to the side to have a man to man talk.

"Wait Benny, hold up bruh". Danny caught up with Benny in the hallway.
"Yeah, what's up." Benny wasn't in the mood to do much talking, but he decided to hear him out. After all, he was deceived by Jovita too.

"Look man, I know this is tougher on you than it is on me ya dig. But man, that's still your son. No matter what, you have been in his life since he was born. Nothing should change after this. When he is old enough, maybe all three of us can sit down and have a heart to heart talk with him. Despite of what his trifflin' ass mama did, that's still your seed. He just got my blood and DNA. I will come around to check on lil man like I always been doing, playing uncle D and shit, but he is your son. Like a man, I don't wanna take that away from you dawg."

"I appreciate that man. This shit kinda' fucking me up right now bruh. Man, this bitch laid up there and had me thinking lil man was mine. I'm just happy it's you bruh and not some other random ass nigga ya know? We wouldn't have no time trying to figure out where he can get blood from. Look, I feel what you sayin' but I'ma need some time to let all this shit sink in. When that doctor told me we wasn't a match, man I 'bout lost it 'cause I knew that only meant one thing; he wasn't my son. Then he got my name and shit? Man, I can just go in there and beat the fuck outta' Jovita bruh." Thinking about the bullshit she pulled pissed Benny off all over again.

"Oh believe you me, I know exactly how you feel. Imagine getting a fucking call saying lil man was my son. Then I goes to the clinic to do a DNA test, and as sure as hell is hot, according to those papers, lil man is my son. That was 'bout 2 years ago bruh. I told her to tell you, but I should have known better. I should have come to you with it myself. I just didn't want to confuse Jr. so I just kept playing the uncle D role ya heard me."

"I feel ya bruh. But wait, when y'all got this DNA test done? I was wondering why that bitch changed her mind about increasing my child support. I wasn't with that shit. I told her we got a fight on our hands cause I wasn't paying her ass no more than what she was already getting from me. So the people told me that we needed a DNA test and she changed her mind all of a sudden. When we had him, we didn't need no blood test. We just had to sign some paper work saying he mine, or something like that. You know a nigga don't know nothing about all this child support bullshit. Now it all makes since. That dirty bitch. She got me though, I can't even front."

"Man that hoe let the whole New Orleans run up in here. She played everybody. She probably had all them niggas thinking they got her ass knocked up. I was fucking her for a while. I slipped up and didn't put a rubber on. Nigga was full of that liquor; you know how that go."

Danny and Benny chatted for a few more minutes, dapped each other off and went back into the waiting where.

****

Back in the waiting room, Jovita was rolling a piece of paper in her hand while staring at the floor.
"What's this?" Benny asked as he snatched the paperwork out her hand.
"Damn Benny, really nigga? Gimme' back my paper." She stood up to get the paper but Benny mushed her forehead and she fell back in her seat.
"If you know like I know, you better stay yo' ass the fuck away from me Jovita."

He unrolled the paper and read the details. "Oh, wow. Look bruh, these look familiar to you?" Benny passed the papers to Danny.

"Fuckin' well right, that's the fuckin' DNA results. I got those same fuckin' papers at the crib. You mean to tell me, yo stupid ass was walking around with the shit in your purse the whole time?" Danny couldn't do nothing but shake his head.

"Look, I'm sorry ok. Yeah, I told Benny he was the daddy 'cause I really thought he was. Then he started to look like you and I knew it was a possibility that you may be his biological father. Y'all both have dimples so it kinda' threw me off. But don't sit here and act like y'all so fuckin' perfect! Benny, you was fucking me, raw, while you was with Shante'. And you Danny, you was fucking me too. Yes, we used protection and all the first time we messed around. But not the second time and it only takes one time to get pregnant." Jovita pleaded her case.

"So why me? Why try and trap me? You got me thinking he is my son, knowing damn well it was a possibility that Danny was the father, too? I know what it is. You only did that shit to get Shante' mad. You thought by me poppin' a baby in ya that we was gon' be on some Jack and Jill type shit? Save that shit you talkin'. You only sorry yo' trifflin' ass got caught!"

Jovita remained quiet. She didn't have shit to say.

Just then the doctor came back into the room with good news. The surgery went well and now Benny Jr. is just resting and recovering. Everyone was happy to hear the good news. Right now, it was all about making sure Benny Jr. was ok.

****

"Yo Gina, where you at bae?" Jeremy came home 2 hours early from the gym. He decided he wanted to surprise her and take her out to eat.

"Gina." He yelled her name, walking around the house. Still no answer. He went into the bedroom and saw that she left a note:

"Hey baby, sorry I went out to eat with some friends. I got you a TV dinner in the freezer. I will see you when I make it back home. Don't wait up. Love you."

"Well ain't this 'bout a bitch. Now when I wanna' chill with her ass, she ain't even home." He decided to give Tracy a call.
He called Tracy's phone but there was no answer. "Damn." He decided to put his dinner in the microwave and take a quick shower while he food heat up.

He went in the living room to eat and watch TV. He heard a chirp noise but didn't know where it was coming from. So, he ignored it.
When he heard it again, he mute the TV to hear where that annoying noise was coming from.

"That shit drivin' me." He mumbled under his breath.
"Chirp". The sound was coming from the laptop. It was a notification sound.
"I told her ass 'bout leaving that damn computer on all night."
He got up and grabbed the laptop and put in their password. He saw that there were 4 of those annoying pop ups.

He was about to close the laptop, until something caught his attention.
He saw that Gina was still logged on to Myspace. So letting his curiosity get the best of him, he decided to snoop through her page. He saw that she post plenty of pictures of her birthday party. He also saw lots of pictures of them together. He didn't think anything of it.

Then he heard the chirp noises again, indicating that Gina had a new message. He clicked on the folder and saw that it was from one of her old high school friends.

As he keep reading through the messages, he came across a familiar face. He could see the small icon of what looked like Tony's profile picture. He decided to click on it. And sure enough, it was the same guy that he saw his wife hugging at her birthday party. He had a funny feeling about Tony, and he was about to find out just how right he was.

He went back into the message folder and decided to click on the messages between Gina and Tony. He saw that they have been sending messages back and forth for a while now. He scrolled down to the very first message that Tony sent her:

Hey, my old neighborhood friend. I was just browsing through Myspace ya' heard me and I came across ya' page. How you been? I see ya' still looking good girl. I hear you got married right after high school. Congrats to you and the Mr. How's the married life though? Me, well I'm still single, with no kids. Life is good on my end. I can't complain. Well I don't wanna' take up too much of your time. But hit me up sometimes or whenever you get a chance. Holla back."

T.

Then he heard Gina's reply:

"Hey Tony. How are you? I am doing fine. You are looking good yourself I see. Damn how tall are you now? You 'bout as tall as Shaq! As for the married life, it's great. I am happy. Well, it was nice of you to hit me up. Make sure you stay in touch. Oh, and before I forget, I am having a party tomorrow night at the hall in the East. So, if you are not busy, swing on by! It was nice talking to you. Don't be a stranger old friend. Later."

G.

He continued to read their messages. The more he read, the more he could feel his blood boiling. He came across their most recent conversation, which was earlier that day:

"Hey beautiful G. How you doin' baby girl? Are we still on for today? I hope so 'cause I can't wait to see you. Hit me up."
T.

Gina's respond:

"Hey Tony. Of course. I'm still down if you are. I haven't eaten all day. And I don't know what time Jeremy will be home. Knowing him, he will probably be at the gym. I swear sometimes I think he cares more about that stupid gym than he cares for me. I am so glad that we got in contact. It's always good to have someone that I can talk to. I have friends, but, they have their own lives ya know?"

Tony's respond:

"Some people just don't know what they have; until a nigga like me come scoop you up. I know one thang, I damn sure wouldn't be in no damn gym every night. Knowing I got a beautiful, fine ass woman like you waiting at home for me. But let me ask you something, are you happy G? I know you said you were, but whenever we talk, you seem down and lonely. Talk to me. You know we go way back. You can talk to me about anything."

Gina's respond:

"I mean, don't get me wrong. I love my husband. He is a good man. But I just don't feel first in his like no more. Plus, he has this temper, and sometimes. ….. Never mind. I don't want to talk about him no more. Let's meet up around 6pm. See you then T."

G.

    Jeremy didn't even bother to read Tony's respond. He'd already read enough. He closed the laptop and placed it back on the table. He got up and started walking in circles, talking to himself.
    "The nerve of this bitch. Gon' leave some cheap ass frozen TV dinner for me and go out and eat with this nigga? Ok."

    He grabbed a beer from the fridge and flopped back down to watch TV. He didn't care what was on the screen at the time. His mind was elsewhere and racing with thoughts of Gina and Tony hooking up.

He decided to sit there and just wait for Gina's return home.

    ****

Fancee was sitting in her living room, chilling and rolling a blunt as usual. She decided to call and ask Shante' for a favor.
    She got her cell phone and dialed her number.

"Hey, what's up chick. Look, I need a huge favor, you think you can work for me tomorrow night? I got something to do and I'm not gon' be able to make it. I know you said you wasn't going in tomorrow, just thought I'd ask you for this favor. I'll break bread with you for looking out for me.

"You would? Girl thanks so much. Just be there 'bout 7pm. That's what time Bunny asked me to be there, even though the club don't start poppin' til 'bout 9. Thanks chick. Good lookin' out. Aiight, bye."

Shante' and Fancee ended their phone call.
"Hey, yeah, she gon' be there for 7 but knowing her, she might get there early. You know what do to. Call me when it's done. Bye."

Fancee lit her blunt and laughed to herself. "Karma is a muthafucka".

****

"I had a great time Tony. We should do this more often." Gina and Tony had stayed at the pizza place on Canal St. for about 2 hours. They talked about everything from their childhood to Gina marital issues that she was having with Jeremy. She even opened up about Jeremy's verbal and physical abuse.

"You know you don't have to end the night right now G. I enjoyed my time with you. I can tell you miss feeling special. I saw that smile you wore all night. And I'm happy to be the man to put it there. Whenever you need me, for anything, don't hesitate to call me baby girl. Not every man is like your sorry ass husband. Never let a man put his hands on you, unless he's doing this."

Tony walked over closer to Gina and placed his lips on hers. He thought she was going to pull back but to his surprise, she didn't. Gina was caught up in the moment, she didn't realize she was kissing Tony out in the open.

"Wait, we can't do this. I'm a married woman. I have a husband at home."

"Who are you trying to convince, me or yourself?"

"Can we go somewhere more private? It's not a good idea to be out in the open."

"How 'bout my place?" "Ok." She agreed and they were on their way.

CHAPTER 17:
KARMA'S MISHAP

"Make sure you call me when you make it home safe. I can't wait to see you again. Remember what I said, I'm always here for you Pretty G." He placed another kiss on her lips and held her tight in his arms for a few seconds.

"Thank you for an amazing night Tony. I will make sure to take you up on that offer." She looked into his eyes and saw stars. She haven't felt like this about another man, besides her husband.

Her husband; the minute she thought of him, she knew she had to make up an alibi about staying out, and fast.

"I gotta go. I will call you when I make it home. Thanks again Tony." They kissed again before she drove off.

****

The morning sun was blazing through her car window. She was about 2 miles away from her home. She decided to stop at McDonalds to get herself and Jeremy some breakfast.

When she got closer to her house, she gave Tony a call to let him know that she made it home safe. She sure in hell wasn't about to call him from her house.

She pulled up to their drive way and parked inside of the garage. She gathered her purse, along with their breakfast and headed towards the living room.

"Hey baby, I'm home. Where you at?"

"WHACK!" For a minute, she saw stars and almost lost track of whereabouts. But those second set of punches to her face knocked her back into reality; Jeremy had just 2-pieced her ass.

"You low down, dirty, cheating ass bitch!" Jeremy slapped Gina about 3 more times until she hit the floor again.

"You think I don't know about you and that nigga Tony? Yeah that's right bitch, I saw those lil messages back and forth from that pussy ass nigga on ya' Myspace! So you fuckin' this nigga now Gina? That's why that nigga was all over you and shit at the party? You on here telling this nigga I don't spend time with you. Bitch I work to pay these bills and take care of yo ungrateful ass!"

He kicked her in her stomach.

"Jeremy please stop! You hurtin' me. I told you I was sleepin' by my friend house. Didn't you get that note I put on the bed?"

"That fuckin' note didn't say shit about you sleepin' out. You was with that nigga! Don't play me for no fool Gina, or I'ma pound the fuck outta' yo' lyin' ass some mo'. And when I see that bitch ass nigga Tony, he gon' be lookin' down the barrel of my 9! Believe that shit. How long you been fuckin' this nigga? And don't lie either bitch!"

"It's not even like that Jeremy. Me and Tony grew up together. That's it! You trippin' for nothin'." Gina cried and sobbed, hoping that he would have sympathy for her being in so much pain.

"Oh so you still lyin' for this nigga ha? Hold up. Stay yo ass right there!" Jeremy stormed to their bedroom. Gina knew when Jeremy got angry, even Satan himself was no match for him. She took this time to struggle to her feet. She grabbed her purse and car keys and hurried to the garage as fast as she could while still in pain. She needed to get away from Jeremy, or today would be her last day on earth.

She got in her car, pressed the lock all button and started the engine. She looked up and saw Jeremy coming towards her car.

"Open this muthafuckin' door Gina, or I'ma break this fuckin' glass."
Gina didn't even wait until the garage door was fully opened. She put her car in reverse and mashed the gas. She tore half of the garage door off trying to get away from Jeremy. She didn't care, better the garage getting tore up than her face.

She reached for her phone and dialed his number.

"Tony, I'm on my way. Jeremy just beat my ass."

"Come straight over here baby, I got you." He waited up for her and swore to beat the breaks off Jeremy for hitting her.

****

Shante' was in the mirror, getting her hair prepared for tonight. She had plans on staying indoors Saturday night and watch some horror flicks, until Fancee called her yesterday and asked to work her shift because they would be short of girls. She didn't mind so she agreed.

When she pulled up to the club, she saw that where wasn't many cars in the parking lot. It was 6:30 but she didn't have to be there until 7pm. She always come to work at least 30 minutes early to give her enough time to prep for her performance.

Instead of going straight inside of the club, she decided to call and check on Benny. She called the number on the card that he'd given her at the mall.

"Hey, this Benny, leave your name and number at the beep and I'ma get back with 'cha. Peace." "Beep."

"Hey Benny, this is Shante'. I was just calling to check on you. I heard about what happened to Benny Jr. and wanted to see if he was ok. Give me a call back whenever you get this message. Later."

As she was placing her cell phone back in her purse, she noticed this all black Crowne Victoria car circling the parking lot. She thought maybe he was trying to get a spot closer to the door. That's until they parked directly behind her.

"Now all these fuckin' parking spots and this muthafucka wants to park right behind me. So fuckin' annoying. Lawd." That was a pet peeve of hers. "Let me get my ass in this club. Get this damn night over with. This my last damn time volunteering to work for somebody else."

As she stepped out of her car, she noticed the driver of the black car opened their door too. She didn't look back to see who it was. She was just ready to get her night over with. Just as she was reaching the entrance of the club, she help a sharp pain in her back, and a hand around her throat.

"Turn around and I'ma parallelize yo' ass. Walk to the back of the club. Hurry up bitch." The aggressor led Shante' to where the dumpsters were towards the back door of the club.

"Now take off your clothes, and you bet not even think about screamin'."

"Look, whoever you are, I have money. You can take it. Please just let me go and I won't tell nobody what happened. You don't have this to do. Please let me go." Shante' was begging for her life. She made up her mind that tonight would be her last night at the club. She would just find another way to make extra money for school. This shit wasn't worth losing her life over.

"Konk!" He punched Shante' in the back of her head with the butt of his knife and she feel to the ground. "Bitch I said, take off your clothes, and shit the fuck up. After all these years, yo' ass is still hard headed."

She was dazed and confused, but she heard his exact words: ***After all these years."*** While trying to get back to her feet, she tried to put two and two together. "Who, who are you? What do you want from me?"

"Oh, so you don't recognize my voice ha, well let's see if you can recognize this."

Just then, the aggressor pulled down his pants and exposed his reattached, deformed looking penis.

"You remember, 1987, when you damn near sliced my whole dick off. Yeah. Thanks to you, I never used the muthafucka' again. Surgery after surgery, and they still couldn't fix my shit. I don't even have feelin' in this muthafucka no mo', and it's all thanks to you. Well tonight, it's time for me to get MY revenge."

"Oh….my… god…. Frank?" All of those memories of her came rushing back. She couldn't believe he found out where she worked. He was the pizza man that delivered the pizza to her house. After Danny pistol whipped him, she thought she'd saw the last of Frank. Yet here he was, standing over her, carrying a knife, with his dick out.

"Like I said, you gon' finish what you started, and I'ma leave yo' ass back here stankin' with the rest of this trash."

He grabbed Shante' by her hair and punched her back to the ground. "Get up bitch! You ain't got all that mouth now ha? Had a lot of shit to say back then. Talk that shit nah." He kicked her again on her side. Get up!"

Shante' was in so much pain. Unlike 12 years ago, she didn't have anything to fight back with. Or so she though. She didn't know if her guardian angel was by her side that night, but she happen to look under the dumpster and saw this nice sized rock. She wasn't gonna' let Frank rape then kill her. Not tonight. She slowly crawled closer to the dumpster, never taking her eyes off that rock. She could still hear Frank in the background talking shit, but she tuned him out. All she saw was her way out; that big ass rock.

She struggled to her feet, and slowly turned around. Just as she did when she was 10, she held that rock in her right hand, and swung hard as she possibly could, and knocked Frank upside his head. He dropped the knife and fell on his back.

Shante' blacked out. Flashbacks of him molesting her and Gina clouded her judgement. She flashed out on Frank. She sat on top of him, grabbed his knife, and commenced to stabbing him. She didn't stop until she saw his eyes roll in the back of his head.

After she came to from her black out, she rolled over on her side and cried. She cried for all the pain he caused her and her sister. She cried for all the hurt and anger that he caused her and her mother. She hated Frank. She looked over at his dick. "It's time I finish was I start 12 years ago. Sick son of a bitch!"

She grabbed the knife she used to stab him, and sliced his dick, completely off this time. Blood shot everywhere, but she didn't care. She should have finished him off 12 years ago.

She got up and walked in the club. "Oh my God, Rain, are you ok? Someone call the police!" One of the dancers yelled out frantically. Shante' (Rain) burst out in tears and waited in the back room for the police.

****

Moments after NOPD arrived on the scene, the crime lab came to pick up Frank's body.

"Mrs. Jenkins, I am Detective Green and this is my partner, Detective Campbell. We know it's not a good time for you right now, but we would like for you to come downtown to answer some questions. If you're up to it."

"Damn the girl was attacked and damn near lost her life and y'all muthafuckas wanna question her? Hello?! She's the fuckin' victim here!"

Bunny was furious with the cops. Shante' was still a bit shaken up but she was ready to cooperate with the detectives.

"It's ok Bunny. I'm good. Let's go detective. Wait, let me call my mama 'nem first so they could meet me downtown."

"Sure." Said the detective.

Once they made it to the police station, Detective Green wasted no time with his interrogation. He offered her something to drink but she declined. She was ready to get those questions over with so she can go home and wash Franks blood from her body.

"Ok, start from the beginning. You went to work, got there at about 6:30, and what happened?"

Shante' explained what went down from the time she pulled up, to the time they were called after she killed Frank. She explained to the detective that Frank had molested her and her sister Gina while they were kids. She also let him in on what she did to Frank as pay back. After learning what such a sick bastard Frank was, he kind of felt sorry for her. He decided to lighten up on the questioning. For all he cared, Frank got just what he deserved.

"Ms. Jenkins, how long have you worked at the gentlemen's club?"

"Look, I worked there for over a year now. I am saving up to go back to school to obtain my degree in Criminal Justice. I have a day job but I wanted to make some extra cash on the side. I wasn't even due to work tonight. I was only there do work for a friend. It wasn't even my night to work. I was doing her a favor."
"And who might this friend be and how long have you known them?"
"I've only known Fancee for about a month now. She cool people. That's who I was supposed to work for tonight."

"Well, Ms. Jenkins, we found the victim's wallet. He had a few pictures inside, along with your address. Would you happen to know this female?" The detective slid the picture of Frank and some girl sitting on his lap.

At a first glance, she couldn't tell who the female was. The picture seemed to be about 10 years old and it had wear and tear from being in the wallet. "We also obtained his phone, and noticed that he have been calling the same number all week. Do you know a person named Felicia?"

"No, not that I know off. Where is all this coming from? I don't know who that is and I don't care. I'm just ready to get home. Are we almost done here officer?"

"Sure, just one more thing. Can I see your phone Ms. Jenkins?"
Shante' handed her phone to the detective. He pulled out Frank's phone and compared a specific number that Shante' had in her phone.

Just as he thought, Fancee and Felicia numbers were the same. He showed them to Shante'. She wore a confused look on her face and grabbed the photo again off the table. This time, she recognized the girl in the photo that was sitting on Franks lap. It was Fancee!

"What the fuck? But how, wait...." She had so many questions at once. The room started to spin of the thought of Frank and Fancee, or Felicia, even knowing each other. This didn't make any sense to her. Why would Fancee be calling Frank?

"You see Ms. Jenkins, here's the deal. We believe that your friend, Fancee, set this whole thing up. First, just out of curiosity, do all the dancers at the club have work schedules? I've always thought you came and danced whenever you wanted to. And knowing that the club doesn't get crowded until around 9pm, doesn't it seem like a coincidence that she would even ask you to come to the club, 2 hours early? Think about it. She knew that there wouldn't be a lot of people there, and that would be the perfect time for Frank to attack you. You said he drove his car around the parking lot a few times, right? And you told me what you've done to him when you were only 10 years old. It seems to me that he's been plotting his revenge on you all along, and using his own daughter to do so."

Detective Green was right on point about everything that transpired that night. It was a set up.

"Are you sure that she's Frank's daughter? I never knew Frank even had kids. But what you are saying kinda' makes sense. Frank even knew where I lived. But Fancee never been to my house so how would he even know that information officer? This is all just too much to take in. I can't believe Fancee, Felicia, whatever the bitch name is, would do me like this. If it wasn't for me finding that rock when I did, I probably wouldn't even be here."

"Where's my baby? Are you ok Shante'?" Pam ran to her daughter and embraced her. She arrived at the police station with both Evan and Joyce. Joyce and Pamela were on the phone together when Pamela got the call that Shante' was attacked and to come downtown.

"Yeah mama, I'm fine. It was Frank. He found me. I had to…" Shante' broke down in her mama arms.

"Where is that muthafucka?! I'ma kill his ass!" Evan was furious.

"We're afraid that won't be necessary sir. Frank is dead. He tried to attack Shante' and she fought back."

"Baby girl, what happened? How did he know how to find you?" Evan asked his daughter.

Before Shante' could even answer, Detective Campbell chimed in. "Sir, your daughter was attacked at the gentlemen's club where she works." He then went into details about what took place at the club with Frank and informed them of Frank's daughter Felicia's involvement.

"Man, you gotta' be mistaken. My daughter don't work at no damn strip club. Is what this man is saying true Shante'?" Evan looked to Shante' for answers.

"Yes daddy! I work at the club to save up for school. It's no big deal. After tonight, I won't be returning back though."

"No big deal? I don't want no child of mine, shakin' her ass for cash. You too got damn smart for that shit Shante'! Baby if you needed extra money, you know you could have come to me. I can't believe you Shante'!"

"Oh, so it's ok for YOU to go to that same club, and having all those dancers all over you? Yeah, that's right daddy. I caught you there twice. So, don't come up in here judging me. Unlike you, I'm there for a purpose and that's to make money. You go there to trick! Now we all know where you be when you don't go home at night!" She turned and looked at her mother and saw the hurt and pain in her eyes, once again, due to her father.

By now both Frank and Shante' were having an all-out screaming match. It can be heard outside of Detective Green's office. An NOPD officer came in to see what all the commotion was about. "Is everything ok in here?"

"Chad?"
"Shante'."

Hey, I didn't know you were a cop. Yeah, everything is ok, I was just about to leave." Shante' gathered her things to leave. "Look, I answered all of your questions, now can I leave, please?"

"Sure, but we will be in touch." Said Detective Green.

"Do you need a ride home? I'm about to get off the clock now. I can give you a ride." Chad offered Shante' a ride home.

"Sure, that would be fine. I damn sure don't ride with in the car with my daddy. Just take me home please. I had a very long night." Chad and Shante' left the police station and headed to her home. During the ride, she filled him in on everything that took place that night.

****

Fancee was at home, waiting on her father's call. It's been over 12 hours and still, she haven't heard from him. She called his phone about 10 times and each time, it went straight to voicemail.

"Where the fuck is he?" She was pacing back and forth, smoking a cigarette. Her nerves was bad and she begin to worry.

A few minutes later, there was a knock at the door.
"This better be his ass." She said to herself. She put her cigarette out and walked to the front door.

She looked through the peephole and saw two black males, both dressed in suits. She opened the door with a twisted look on her face.

"Hello ma'am. I am Detective Green and this is my partner, Detective Campbell. We would like to ask you a couple of questions. May we come in?"

"Umm, hell no. I don't do cops so whatever you need to ask me, you can ask me right on the outside. So, what's up? What might you need from me?" She stood in the doorway with her arms folded, looking back and forth between both officers.

"Well ma'am, since you put it that way. Then let's get right to the point. Is your name Felicia Jones and do you also go by the name, Fancee?"

"Yeah, and? Wait, how you even know my name?"

"We will answer any questions that you may have, but first, we need you to come with us."

"Go with y'all for what?" She was becoming agitated.

"Ms. Jones, we need you to come to the morgue to identity a body. We think it may be your father."

CHAPTER 18:
SEALED WITH A KISS.

A week has passed since the night that Shante' was attacked. She decided to take the rest of the week off from her day job to relax her mind. She still wasn't quite over the events that took place that night. It was like a recurring nightmare. She even started seeing Frank in her sleep. Even in death, he still seemed to be a pain in her ass.

She got up, fixed breakfast and decided she would just lay in bed all day. She still hadn't heard anything from the detectives and not to her surprise, she didn't hear from Fancee, either. She still couldn't believe that Fancee befriended her, knowing she had other plans on her agenda. She vowed to herself that she will be more careful about who she called her "friends".

She was heading to the kitchen to put away her dishes until she heard a knock at the door.

"Hey mama, what you doin' here?"

"Shante', get dressed, we are going for a ride. I will explain everything later." Pam seemed a bit angry but shaken. Shante' was curious about her mother's behavior. She never saw this side of her.

"Umm ok. Just let me put some clothes on right quick."

****

"Mama, why are we at Aunt Fay's house?"

Pamela didn't answer. She just got out of the car and banged on her sister's door.

"Who the fuck is it?" Fay yelled. She swung the door open; looking high as hell. "What in the fuck is wrong with... Well I'll be damned. Hey there, Pamela. What brings you here?" She looked over at Shante'. She didn't say hello but she damn sure had a bone or two to pick with her.

"And why yo' Kill Bill ass over here? Last time I saw you, you was cuttin' dick off. You got some nerves showin' yo' face at my damn house." She barked at Shante'.

Shante' was about to say something but Pamela intervened.

"Fay, some shit went down with my baby last Saturday, and I am sure you knew all about it. Tell me something Fay, how come you never mentioned Felicia? It's bad enough you knew that son of a bitch was molesting my daughters and didn't do shit about it, but why go so far Fay?"

"First of all, getcha' story straight. I don't know nothin' 'bout what Frank and Felicia tried to do to her at that damn club. You barkin' up the wrong fuckin' tree today. You need to go talk to them muthafuckas. I ain't got shit to do with shit."

"See, I find that very hard to believe. I never mentioned in detail what took place. So that lets me know that you know exactly what the fuck I am talking about! You keep lyin' to me, and you gon' end up in the morgue right along with his ass!"

"What you mean, morgue?" That statement grabbed Fay's attention.

"Oh, you didn't know. That muthafucka tried to attack Shante' but she stopped his ass, just like she did 12 years ago. But this time, he won't be recovering."

"You BITCH!" Fay tried to run up on Shante', but not before Pamela gave her a good right hook. Fay fell her fragile ass on her coffee table.

"I wish the fuck you would try to lay your hands on my child. If anybody need their ass beat is you. Growing up, I knew you was gonna' turn out to be an evil, low down bitch. But I would have never thought in a million years that you would hurt my children. You lettin' him get away with what he's been doing is just as worst as him doing it. You belong right in hell with his ass."

Fay had a few words of her own. She was so high, she didn't even try to get off the broken coffee table glass. She just laid there, looking half dead.

"You always thought you were better than me Pamela. We had different daddies and because of that, we got different treatments. Mama always thought highly of you and looked down on me like I wasn't shit all because my daddy wasn't shit. I didn't ask to come here and I shouldn't have been treated no differently from you 'cause we both come out the same pussy. So yeah, I had it out for you, so what? That's the outcome of playing favoritism. But since you wanna' come up in my damn house and look down on me, why don't you tell Edward Scissor hand over there all about your little secrets."

Fay carried on. "See, I know I ain't shit, but I don't hide it. I lay all my cards out on the table. I don't have secrets. But 'cha see you, you want everybody around yo stuck up ass to think you this perfect mother and perfect little wife. But you ain't no fuckin' better than me. You only better at hidin' the shit. So, let me ask YOU somethin', does Evan know about your secrets? Did you tell him about Frank so called molesting your daughters? It's funny that he never stepped foot in my house after the last time I saw you. I know at any given time Evan would have snapped Frank's neck for what he did to them. So yo ass didn't tell him shit. You know why? 'Cause you wanna keep up that perfect image of yours. Maybe I should let him in on all your little secrets." Fay laughed while lighting up a cigarette.

"Mama, what is she talkin' about?" By now, Shante' was all ears. She needed to know what secrets her mother was holding back from her. "Aunt Fay, what are you talkin' about?"

"Ask ya' mama. She knows. Now if y'all don't mind, y'all need to get the fuck out my house."

As they were leaving, Pam turned and had a few words for her sister. "May God have mercy on your soul. From this day forward, you are dead to me."

The ride back to Shante's place was quiet. All sorts of things were running through her mind about her mother having secrets. Pam dropped Shante' off and was headed home.

****

Shante' was back at home, getting some much-needed rest and watching TV. Lately, her phone has been ringing off the hook. Most of them were from blocked calls. She even tried to *67 the calls but with no success. Her phone rang again but she decided to let it go straight to voicemail.

Someone started knocking at her door. She wasn't expecting any visitors today so she wondered who that could be.

"Who is it?"

She didn't wait for an answer. She opened the door without looking through the peephole and was met with a 9-millimeter pointed at her face and a very pissed off Fancee aka Felicia Jones.

She stumbled as she took a step back. She raised both her hands. "Fancee, what you doin' at my house? Please put the gun down. Let's talk; you don't have to do this." Once again, she found herself begging for her life. Not too long ago she had to beg Fancee's father Frank and now this bullshit? When will enough be enough, she thought.

"Shut up and move. Plant ya' ass on that sofa. Make a slick ass move and I'ma blow ya' fuckin' face off bitch!" Fancee was giving orders while keeping her finger on the trigger. She looked like she hasn't slept in days. She even looked a lot smaller than the last time Shante' saw her at the bachelor party.

Shante' was afraid, but at the same time, she was sick and tired of being a victim of Frank's and Fancee's foolishness. After seeing that her pleading wasn't getting through to Fancee, Shante' just let her have it. Something clicked in Shante'. She was tired. If she had to take out Fancee the same way she took out Frank, then so be it. She was tired of begging for her life.

"You know, you got some fuckin' nerve showin' up at my house after that bullshit you pulled last week! You lucky you got that gun, or else I would beat the fuck outta' you. What the fuck do you want Fancee? That gun don't pump no fear in my heart, so if you gon' pull the trigger, then pull it bitch." Shante' stood up, walked over to Fancee and placed the 9 on her forehead. She wanted to pull Fancee's hoe cord. And it seemed to be working. That caught Fancee by surprise. She expected Shante' to be on her knees, crying and begging for her life. That other side of Shante' wouldn't let that happen.

"He was all I had, why did you have to go and take him from me Rain? He was everything to me." To her surprise, Fancee started crying her eyes out but she never took her finger off that trigger. "My daddy was all I had in this world. When my own mama left me for dead, he took care of me. He wasn't perfect but he loved me when she didn't. You didn't have to kill him Rain. He was only gonna' scare you."

"Scare me, bitch is you serious? That nigga tried to KILL ME! You know what I had to go through when I was little? Me AND my lil' sister? That muthafucka you call "daddy" is a fucking child molester! Every chance he got he would come and have his way with me and my sister!"

"SHUT UP! I don't wanna' hear no mo'!" Fancee covered her ears while still holding on to the gun.

"No, you need to hear this shit! That muthafucka deserved what I did to him 12 years ago and now he deserves to be right where the fuck he at right now; 6 feet deep! Do you know how it felt, being helpless while you watched your little sister being raped against her own free will? He shovin' his dick in every hole that he could fit his dick in and didn't care that she was bleedin' and cryin' her heart out for him to stop. I had to watch that shit! I couldn't even help my own lil' sister against that fuckin' sick monster that YOU call a daddy! Let me ask you somethin' Fancee, did Frank ever touch you?"

"Stop it Rain. I told you I don't wanna hear no more."

"ANSWER ME! Did Frank ever molest you Fancee? Because if he can do it to me and my sister, I know he did it to you too. Especially being that your mama wasn't around. He had no one to stop him."

"WHACK! I told you to SHUT THE FUCK UP! He was all I had!" Fancee hit Shante' upside her head with the butt of her gun. Shante' grabbed the side of her head and fell to her knees. "Say one more thing and this time I'ma splatter yo' fuckin' brains all over this muthafucka'."

"Go head, do it! Do what the fuck you came to do." Shante' stood to her feet. "You can pistol whip me, hell, you can even blow my brains out, but I refuse to die on my knees. I know Frank touched you. I saw the look in your eyes when I asked you. What would you have done if you knew he was doing what he did to me and my little sister, to your sister or daughter? How would you feel hearing your baby girl crying out for help? What would you do? Frank was your father but Frank was a monster Fancee. I ain't even mad at you for setting me up. Frank has a way of makin' people do what he wants them to do. My aunt heard our cries but she never came to our rescue. Yes, my own aunt let Frank molest us. I know he left out the part of why I had to do what I had to do as a 10-year-old girl. I had to protect myself and my sister. I was only a child when your father raped me; stole my innocence. Stole my sister's innocence. I would not wish that on nobody. Not even you. Frank wasn't right Fancee. No child should have to go through what Frank put us all through. I don't blame you. I even forgive you. Just please, put the gun down. You have a chance to live a good life and not have to worry about being a spawn in Frank's army. You have a chance to make a difference but if you pull that trigger, you are no better than Frank."

By now, Fancee was crying up a storm. She knew that Shante' was right about everything that she'd said. Frank molested her just about every day. He even told her that all fathers did this to their daughter. He made her trust him. He made her feel like if she didn't go along with him, he would leave her just like her mother did. She knew that fathers and daughters shouldn't have sex, but she was so afraid of being left alone, so she went right along with it for a long time. She was being molested by her father so much that it became the norm. She even became pregnant with his baby but she knew she couldn't keep it. So, Frank made her abort it. He put her through hell at such a young age. He even made her turn trick to support his drug habit. Compared to what she went through, Shante' and Gina had it easy.

"I'm so sorry Rain." It was Fay. She help set it up. She was the one that told my daddy where you stayed. The night he bought that pizza over here, he attacked the dude and took his shirt. He ended up puttin' him in the hospital. I feel so bad. I didn't know he did that to you. He just told me you cut him 'cause you was evil. But I should have known better. I guess he had me fooled too. I feel so fuckin' stupid." She started to cry again. She put the gun down and gave Shante' a big hug.

"It's ok. Let it all out. It's not your fault. We are all victims here. Just let it out." Shante' started rubbing her back and wiped her own tears away.

After their crying episode, her and Fancee sat down and talked about her past. She told her things that Frank had her doing and it bought tears to Shante's eyes. Just when she thought that her and Gina were going through the Frank Blues alone, his own daughter had it 10 times worst. She was so happy that Shante' had forgiven her. After all, she had no one is left to care for her.

****

Knock, knock. "UPS! Can you sign for this letter ma'am?" Pamela signed for the package and closed the door.

"Now who sends off a letter with no return address?" The letter only had her address and on the back of the envelope was a lip print; as if the letter was sealed with a kiss. "What type of shit is this?"

She sat on the living room sofa and opened the envelope. Inside was a 2-page letter, all written in red. "And who in the hell writes in red?" Pamela asked herself. She unfolded the letter and read on:

"Hey Barbara, this is Shirley. Ha! No not really, but since I ain't much of a singer, this letter should do the trick."

"To whom it may concern, Pamela Jenkins, I'm writing to you to let you know that honey, we share somethin' in common. Take a wild guess. If you guessed your husband, then you are smarter than I give you credit for. Yes honey, we've been sharing the same man for a very, very long time."

Pam threw the letter on the coffee table and covered her mouth. After reading those lines, she felt like the world took a shit on her chest. Her chest felt heavy. She closed her eyes and tried to gather herself. "Okay, Okay." She did her breathing exercise to calm herself down. She picked up the letter and continued to read:

"Knowin' you, your mouth probably wide open. I can see the dumb look on your face right now. Yep. That's the same damn look I had when I found out that Evan not only stayed with you, but never had any intentions on leaving you to be with me; correction, to be with us! That's right. We have a child together. A handsome son. He is 22, same age as your oldest daughter. So that means, we were both pregnant at the same time. Ain't that somethin'?

Yeah but back to Evan. I swear that man could do some things with my body. No man has ever made me feel the way he does. No wonder yo' ass don't wanna' let him go even after he been cheatin' on ya'. Shit I wouldn't either. Humph. What a man, what a MAN!

But back to me and you. See, we have a problem here. I have been layin' low and now I am tired of being in this hidden place. I've waited for almost 22 years to be with your husband, my man. While he pampered you, and played father to your children, he had me raise our son all along. Do you know how that made me feel? Seeing y'all all hangin' out like one big fake ass Brady Bunch family, while me and my son is kept in the dark?

I blame you for everything I have been through! You the damn reason why I'm not happy, and haven't been happy since the day I found out about yo ass! Why you gotta' be so damn clingy? Why won't you just leave so we can be a family? Can't you tell by now that he don't wanna' be with you? He only stayed that long because of the kids. He didn't want child support to hit him up. Now that they are grown, there is no need to still be with you or in that marriage.

I mean damn girl; all the signs are in your damn face! He come home late or he don't come home at all, plus he ain't even fuckin' you! Yet yo' ass just won't leave! I am sure you will find a nice guy. All these single men out here, one of 'em will feel sorry for you and scoop you up. Hell, be with a damn woman for all I care. Just leave me and Evan be!

I know you don't have a clue of who I am, but I promise you. In due time, you will. My pretty little head will surface sooner than you think. See you soon, soon to be ex-wife.

Signed,

Future Mrs. Jenkins

She couldn't believe what she was reading. Not only did Evan cheat on her for over 22 years, but he allegedly had an outside child with this mystery woman. Instead of crying like she would normally do, Pamela grew angry. She was a damn good woman and she put up with so much bullshit from Evan. Staying out late, not coming home, scratches on his back and now this bullshit? Hell no! Enough was enough! She decided that today will be the day that she put Evan in his place. Once and for all. Until then, she called her friend to fill her in on the letter she'd received.

"Hello? Hey girl, what's goin' on witcha?" Joyce was overjoyed to receive the phone call. She knew that the letter finally reached its destination. She made sure to get a required signature from UPS. She wanted to make sure someone got it; preferably Pamela.

Just like a canary, Pamela wasn't no time in telling Joyce all about the letter. She pretended to be so caring and concerned; knowing that she was the author of that same letter.

"Girllll, wait! Fa' true? Who could the letter come from?"

"Joyce if I knew, I would be knockin' at that bitch's door right about now! I can't believe this disrespectful ass bitch been fuckin' with MY husband! And for 22 years? Joyce this bitch had the cheek enough to tell me to leave my own damn husband. What type of shit is that?" Pamela was heated.

"Damn Pamela. Girl I never saw this side of you. But why do it seem like you only mad at the woman? Isn't Evan the real blame? I mean, it does take two to tangle ya' know? It ain't all her fault. He promised that woman that he would be with her and she pissed off that he reneged on that promise. So, you ain't the only one he hurt. She hurt too. You should be mad at his ass, not her. She only did what any scorned woman would do."

"Whoa hold the hell up, who side you on Joyce? I don't give a fuck if he promised the bitch a clown for her birthday party. He is my husband! The bitch done crossed the line when she sent this damn letter to my house. She got some fuckin' nerve! For all I know, it's all bullshit. What the hell she gotta' be mad for? I'm the one with the title. That bitch obviously didn't mean shit to him cause he still with me and he never did shit for her or her bastard ass son. I don't have no type of sympathy for no woman that's purposely trying to ruin someone else's marriage. Fuck her and her son." Pamela went off!

Joyce had to remain cool and calm because Pamela's words was fucking her up internally. She didn't wanna' blow her cover just yet. She sucked it up and took all the blows that Pamela delivered.

"Look, this ain't about takin' no sides. All I'm sayin' is, it ain't all her fault. Evan is the common denominator in this whole ordeal. So, don't just shot ya gun at that woman and her son. No child asked to be here, regardless of him being born outside of the marriage. You can't bad mouth that child. And if that is his son, as said in that letter, then you would have to except him also. If you love your husband so much. That's all I'm sayin'." Pamela remained quiet. Joyce decided to dig some more.

Joyce continued. "So, what you gonna' do? I still would leave his ass girl. That's too much drama. You don't need that BS nor him. Let her have his ass. It'll be less of a headache for you Chile." Joyce was beyond lowdown. Still trying to convince her to leave her husband.

"It's gon' take more than some letter to make me just up and leave my husband. I need some proof from the bitch." Pamela was hurt but wasn't a fool. She knew how scandalous a woman could be. They would do anything to get your man; even lie and bring up a child in the equation.

"Ok, say you get your proof, then what? You still gon' stay. What if he does leave with her, where does that leave you? Hello? Pamela? You there? Shit!" Joyce hung up and called Pamela back.

When Pamela answered the phone, she can hear her yelling at the top of her lungs. She figured it was Evan who was on the receiving end of Pamela's verbal venom. This was the perfect time to add gas to the fire. She hung up the phone, went to her bedroom closet and retrieved the rest of the evidence. She was on her way to drop the atomic boom on both Evan and Pamela. It had to be done. Too much time has passed as it is. It was time to get her man. She got her house keys and was on her way to the Jenkins resident to stir up some more shit!

****

"Pamela, calm yo' ass down! What fuckin' letter are you talkin' about?!" Evan was ducking vases, frying pans and everything else that Pamela was throwing at him. He'd came home right in the middle of her and Joyce's phone call. She didn't give a damn about what Joyce was talking about; she needed to confront his ass.

"You lyin', cheatin', selfish son of a bitch! After all these fuckin' years I put up with yo trifflin' ass! I knew you been cheatin' on me Evan. I knew that much. And ya' don't even have respect for your own wife. Just like the other night; ya' bring ya' ass home with scratches on ya back and don't lie and say I did it nigga; or I'ma hum this fuckin' lamp at yo head! You damn sure ain't been fuckin' me for the past few months. So, is the bitch in the letter the reason why yo ass never come home at night? And who is this son y'all supposed to have had together? C'mon, I need some answers Evan. You owe me that much."

"Look baby, I am sorry. Things haven't been the same since I had to retire and I was stressed out. I'm sorry for cheatin' on you but it won't happen again. And that letter is bullshit Pamela. I don't know who sent it and I don't have no outside children with her or nobody! Let's just talk this over baby. Calm down."

Seeing Pamela this angry had him spooked. This was the first time that he'd seen his wife raise hell. He couldn't blame her though. He knew eventually he would get caught. He could take Joyce and ring her by her neck. He knew who sent that letter, but he had to play it off. He thought about the time she said he will be getting a package a while back at Shante's graduation party some years ago. He didn't think she would go through with it though. Guess he should have taken her more serious.

Pamela tossed the balled-up letter to Evan. "Here, read this shit for yourself. It came earlier today." He sat in the chair and read the letter. He didn't need to read it but he did. He had to play like he didn't know anything.

"Man, this letter is so full of shit. Why the bitch didn't leave a return address? Come on Pamela, you gotta' be smarter than this."

"You tell me. You the one that's been fuckin' her for 22 years. And you can't be too smart; she found out where the hell you live."

Someone knocked at the door. Pamela got up to answer. It was Joyce. She was carrying a medium sized brown box.

"Oh, did I interrupt somethin'? I just came to check on you girl. I was talkin' on the phone and the call dropped. When I called back I heard you fussin'. Everything good? Do he know about the letter?"

"Don't you have somebody else business to be in, your nosey ass bitch! I'm sick of you showin' yo ass around here. Go find somethin' to do. Let me and my wife handle this. This has nothin' to do with your snoopin' ass."

Just as Joyce was about to snap back at Evan, Gina and Tony came rushing through the door. She wore a black eye and even had a busted lip. "Baby what happened? Who did this to you?" Pamela ran to Gina and embraced her.

"Mama, it was Jeremy. He beat me. He always beatin' me. I went to Tony's house to get away from him. Is it ok if I stay over here for a few days? I can't go back to that house mama. He gon' kill me."

"Yes baby, of course you can." Evan rubbed the back of Gina's head. After this drama with Joyce's letter, he'd decided that he would pay Jeremy a visit for abusing his daughter. He didn't care too much for the bastard anyways.

"Baby, you know you can stay by me if you want to. He liable to find you over here 'cause he knows this is the first place you would go to." Tony said to Gina.

"Baby, what the hell you mean, baby? So, this is the "person" you've been talkin' to son? Oh no, you gotta' cut her off. She off limits." Joyce wasn't having it. She knew why they couldn't be together. And soon they will know too.

"What you mean mama, I gotta cut her off? What did Gina ever do to you?" Tony wasn't feeling what his mama was saying.

"Should you tell them, or should I?" Joyce looked at Evan. She can see the lump in his throat and the sweat beads forming on his forehead.

"Tell them, what?" Pamela asked.

Joyce turned to her son. "Tony, meet your biological father. Evan."

CHAPTER 19:
PRESS PLAY

"What the fuck, did you just say? If I am hearing this correctly, you did just say, that Evan was Tony's father, right?"

"DaDaDid I stutter?! Yeah, you heard me! Evan is my baby daddy! Yes, it was me who wrote you that letter. Tell her Evan. Tell her after all these years, you still want me and not her. Tell her about our plans on being a family after you divorce her ass. Tell her that Tony is your son. Tell her! Don't sit there with that dick look now! I warned you that this was how I was gonna' play my hand, but you took me for to play with. Oh, and just in case you try and deny anything, I brought this. You said you needed proof right Pamela? Where here it all is. Right in this box. Go ahead. See for yourself." She tossed the box to Pamela.

Just as she said, Joyce had all the proof of Evan's infidelity. There were old pictures of her and Evan, coupled up like they were a match made in heaven. She saw the Western Union receipts that Evan has been sending her through the years for her bills and for Tony. And finally, she saw the DNA results. Tony is definitely Evan's son.

Before she was angry. Now she was devastated. She fell to her knees, still with the paper in hand.

"This couldn't be. This just can't be. No, No NO!"

She then looked up at Joyce. "It was you, this whole time Joyce? You befriend me, just to get close to my husband? I opened up to you about everything, and this is the thanks I get for being a good friend to you?" Even though the proof was in her face, she still was in disbelief. This was a living nightmare!

"Save it Pamela! I never said we were friends and I never claimed to be your friend. You are a true definition of a weak woman. You didn't even know me a good month and yet you told me everything that happened and happens under your roof. That's a big mistake. Never tell another woman the dirt on your own husband or your family issues. That's where you fucked up at. The only thing you was ever good for was helpin' me keep tabs on Evan; My man. I even helped get this house. You remember that guy in the hole in the wall, who you was all booed up with? Yeah, he was the one that told me about the rental property; This house that you're living in. So, I had him contact Evan after finding out that y'all had to move out that big ass house in East Over. I have a few friends at that fire station where my man used to work. Sweetie, I BEEN keepin' tabs on y'all. You was never a friend to me. More like a pain up my ass. You want everybody to think you so fuckin' perfect. But you ain't foolin' nobody but yourself."

She turned to Evan. "So baby, did you know that Frank has been molesting your daughters whenever they slept by Fay's house back in the day? Why do you think she quit her job downtown? That's right, she quit so she can watch her own kids because her trifflin' ass sister let that man have his way with Shante' and Gina. I told her that she should tell you, but nooooo. She wanna' keep it in her secret skeleton stashed closet."

"You dirty bitch! I dare you!" Pamela stood up.

"Dare me, double-triple dare me. Your threats don't phase me not one bit. Here you go Evan, take a listen for yourself."

She pulled out a cassette player and handed it to Evan.

"Press play. Hear it for yourself."

Evan pressed play and listened:

Pamela: *"I haven't made the final decision to go back yet, but I'm damn sure thinking about it girl. It's been a long time and this depending on my husband shit just ain't cutting it for me. I need my own money, plus I just miss working. Shante' is old enough to keep an eye on her sister and lil' brother now if need be. Gina ain't too much of a problem. But that son of mine is wild as hell."*

Joyce: *"I feel ya' girl. But you had to stay home after what happened to your girls at 'cha sister's house. But to tell you the truth, Chile you better than me. I would have killed that trifling son of a bitch Frank and ya' sad ass sister. Last I heard, they had to sow his shit back together. Serves him right."*

Pamela: *"Girl don't talk about that shit right now while my husband is in the house. He don't know about what happened and I wanna' leave it like* *that. I've been able to keep them skeletons in the closet all these years and I wanna' leave it like that."*

Joyce: *"Girl my bad shit I didn't know he was home. He must be invisible 'cause I never saw his ass the whole time y'all been staying out here. But back to Frank's ass, I'm just saying. You shouldn't have kept that type of stuff from your husband though. I would've told him. Frank would be one dead mutha fucka if it was up to me. So, when you plan on telling him about you wanting to go back to work?"*

"Click". That was the end of the tape.

Evan didn't say a word. He walked over to the sofa and sat down. He put the tape player on the side of him and put his head down. The word hasn't even been discovered yet to describe the way that he was feeling. He wanted to cry, kill and cry all over again after hearing his own wife withhold that part of his daughters' life from him. Joyce carried on in details about what Shante' did to Frank when she was only 10 years old.

"Pamela. You mean to tell me, you let that son of a bitch get away with molesting my fuckin' daughters, and you didn't think you needed to bring that to my attention? My babies Pamela! My muthafuckin' babies! If that punk muthafucka wasn't already dead, I swear I would have killed him. I should dig his ass up and kill him all over again!"

"I'm sorry Evan. I knew that's what you would have done. That's why I didn't tell you. I didn't want to see you locked up for killin' that bastard. Shante' did damage control to Frank and I figured that was payback enough. I know what I did was wrong, but that doesn't change the fact that you had an outside child on me! Explain that!"

"Fuck that shit Pamela! Yeah, so what? I had another child. Since we being all upfront about shit. I told you in the first place that I wasn't ready to get married. You thought gettin' pregnant with Shante' would change my mind. I was just fine with us just being together. We didn't have to get married for a nigga to stay with you! You basically dragged me to the got damn alter. Givin' me ultimatums and shit. You know I would never let my kids grow up without being in their lives!"

"But what about Tony? Wasn't he important enough for you to be in his life as well? That shit ain't even fair."

"Shut the hell up! Don't even open your mouth. You thought comin' up in here with this bullshit was gon' make me go against my own husband? Well ya' ass thought wrong! Your plan didn't work!" Pamela decided to stand by her man.

"Oh is that right? Well Evan. You need more proof to why you need to leave her? Here you go. She even left her own daughter's party to hang out in the club with this dude she been creepin' with. He's the one that helped with this house that I told you about earlier."

Joyce handed Evan an envelope full of pictures of Pamela and the mystery man from the club after Gina' party. You could see steam forming from Evan's head. He was pissed off to the 10th power.

To everyone's surprise, instead of being angry at his wife, he turned to Joyce and read her like today's newspaper.

"You scandalous, trifflin' ass bitch you. You think I'm stupid ha? This shit looks all too familiar. That's the same shit you pulled with me over 22 years ago. As a matter of fact, Pamela, do you remember what happened that night? Did she offer to buy you a drink?"

"Yeah,. I told her that I wanted a wine cooler while I went to the restroom. I mentioned that it was kinda of strong. You know I've been drinkin' wine coolers for years but they never affected me the way they did that night. Come to think of it, that bitch told me the club drinks have an extra kick to it. I should have known better. Ain't no wine cooler that strong to knock ya out cold and to have me carryin' on the way I did with that man. She had to put somethin' in my drink."

"Yeah that sounds about right. I remember we went out to have drinks. I ordered one damn beer. Next thing I know, I wakes up in her damn bed. Just as naked as a bald pussy. I didn't know what happened. And someone mysteriously took pictures of us. She even took pictures of me being in her bed. She threatened to tell you if I ever tried to leave her. Then four months after that, she told me she was pregnant with Tony.

So you see baby, this bitch was nothin' more than a couple of one-night stands baby. I never had no plans on being with this psycho. She had me by the balls all these years and now you know everything. I'm glad all this shit is out in the open now. Tony is my son. Look baby, I am so sorry for hurtin' you all these years. I can take my lick. I'm guilty of being with her and even fathering her child. But I swear I would never leave you for her. Please forgive me baby. I can become a better man. Just work with me. I take all the blame baby. All of it."

Evan walked over to his wife, got one his knees and like a child begging for candy, he wrapped his arms around her legs. "Let's work this out baby. No more cheatin' and secrets. I promise. I understand the decision you had to make with Frank. You did it to protect our family. Lord knows I would have been in jail right now from taking matters into my own hand. I forgive you for keepin' that secret. I love you."

"I love you too baby. And of course I forgive you. For better or worse, remember our vows? We gonna get through this with God's help." Pamela signaled for Evan to give up. They both cried together.

"Oh no. Evan! After all these years of you promisin' me that you gonna be with me. This bitch been cheatin' on you and she kept shit from you that you needed to know. And all you gotta say about that shit is "Please forgive me?"

"Bitch do you really think that I would leave my wife, and be with your crazy ass? You gone pecans hoe. Get the fuck out of my house and don't 'chu ever show yo' face around here again."

"Evan baby you don't mean that shit. Come on. What about what we shared? You said you loved me, remember?" Now it was Joyce who was doing all the begging and whining.

"You heard him, get out of OUR home. All of that energy you wasted and look at you, you still lose." Pam turned her back to Joyce and stared back at her husband. "I love you baby. We can get through this."

"Oh ah ah. Bitch I done had enough of you." Joyce charged at Pamela and they both fell to the floor. Pamela was caught off guard. Joyce sat on top of her and started landing punches wherever they may fall. Pamela kept her face covered.

"I done had enough of yo' slick ass mouth. Bitch I been waitin' to beat yo ass!" Joyce turned into a mad woman. Gina grabbed Joyce by her hair and yanked her to the floor. "Bitch get the fuck off my mama!" Gina wasn't having it.

Tony grabbed his mother off the floor and Evan helped his wife to her feet.

"I'ma let you have that one bitch. Now square up. Only a weak bitch would attack when ya off guard. Come on Joyce. I'ma give you an ass whippin' that ya mammy should have gave you bitch. You weak ass bitch. Get the fuck out my house."

"Come on mama, let's go! You did even damage for one night." Tony grabbed his mother. She was still talking shit.

"Hey Tony, look son, I'm sorry for not being a part of your life. Your mother, she's a lot to deal with ya know? But still, that shit don't excuse me from missin' out on your life."

"And Tony, you are our family now too. You are my husband's son, so now that makes you my son too."

"Thanks Ms. P. Mr. Evan, I understand, but you still chose not to be a part of my life, so you don't get a free pass patnah. Gina, I'm so sorry." He left out the door, dragging his mother along.

"Unbelievable daddy." Gina shook her head and headed upstairs to her and Shante's old room. She had no words for him. Her mother may have forgiven him that easy, but not her. She was still trying to wrap her head around everything that took place. And Tony is her brother? Only if she would have found this out before they started having an affair.

****

"I really enjoyed myself tonight Chad. After the week I've had, this was exactly what I needed. Thanks for showing me a good time."

Shante' and Chad decided to go on a date. They went to the movies and had dinner afterwards.

"The pleasures all mine. We don't have to end the night just yet. Wanna' come over to my place?"

"Now you know it's unlady like to go to a man's house on the first date. But you can come to my place."

Chad followed her to her place. They stayed up for hours, watching movies and talking about everything under the sun. After being up all day, she fell asleep in his arms.

"Hey sleeping beauty. I guess it's time to call it a night. You all over here snoring and stuff. Let's do this next weekend when I'm off."

She wasn't ready to end their night just yet. "Aww. Do you have to go?" She whined while poking out her lips.

"I gotta' let you get your beauty sleep sweetheart. I know you're tired. I want to be a gentleman."

"I don't want to sleep alone tonight Chad." She grabbed his chin and kissed his lips. He couldn't resist. He decided to stay the night. How can he not? After a kiss like that, she had him at her mercy.

"Let's take it to the bedroom."

"After you princess."

CHAPTER 20:
A FATHER'S BETRAYAL

"Hey Shante', this is Benny. Sorry I haven't gotten back with you at the hospital. Just been a hard week for me. Give me a call back when you get this message. Peace."

Benny tried calling Shante' back a couple of times. The last time he called, he decided to leave a message. Benny Jr. was still in the hospital recovering from his surgery. He was doing much better now. He's able to talk and eat on his own. He still isn't 100% to go home just yet.

Benny was sitting on the end of Jr.'s hospital bed, rubbing his little hand. He imagined what could have been the outcome if Danny wasn't a match. He was happy that he was able to pull through. He hated seeing his son with all those tubes all over his body. But at the same time, he was happy that he survived. He could have easily been planning a funeral right about now.

Danny had called to check on Benny Jr. And after sleeping at the hospital for 3 days, Jovita decided to go home and get some rest. Benny never left his sons' side. He was able to take 2 weeks emergency leave off work.

His cell phone started ringing. It was Shante' returning his call.

"Hey Shante'. Thanks for calling back. How ya doin'?"

"Hey Benny. I am doin' alright. How's lil man holdin' up? I'm so sorry to hear what happened to him. Darlene called and told me the bad news. Do you need anything?" Shante' was being very supportive.

"Nah, I'm good. Thanks for askin' though. Just you callin' to check on me and my son means a lot. Thank you so much. It's still a shocker ya know? Finding out after all these years that he is not my biological son. And Jovita, man, that bitch is evil. She knew Danny was his son the whole time. Me and Danny had a man to man talk. Guess lil man got 2 daddies now ha?"

"I'm so sorry that happened to you. Jovita will get hers. Just continue to be there for your son. He will always be your son. I still haven't talked to Danny yet. So much has happened this past week Benny."

Shante' filled him in on the incident with Frank and his daughter Felicia. She even mentioned her working at the strip club. They talked on the phone for 2 hours. Benny was happy to have her back into his life again; even if it was only as friends.

****

Mark arrived home from picking up their daughter Melody from Nadia's grandmother's house. It was 11am in the morning. Nadia was at work and he had the day off so decided to run a few morning errands.

"Come on daddy baby. Let's get you out of this car seat." He unstrapped Melody and they headed inside.

He fed her, played with her for a little while then he rocked her to sleep for her daily afternoon nap. He decided to surf the web since there was nothing good on TV.

He logged onto his Yahoo email account to check his email. He had over 100 unread messages. It was time he got rid of some of this junk mail. While on his deleting spree, he came across an email with the subject typed in bold red letters. It titled: **Mark Jenkins, Read Immediately and Carefully (No Spam)**

"What's all this about?" He clicked on the email and saw that it had a few attachments. He downloaded them and saved them on his desktop so it can be easily accessible to him.

When he looked over the few documents, he saw that one of them were some adoption papers, according to the title. He decided to check out the other attachments but stopped when he came across the typed letter titled "READ FIRST!", again, in red letters. He maximized the screen and started to read:

"Hey Mark. You don't know me, but I know of you. I won't reveal my identity right now but in due time, you will know who I am. I am very familiar with your family; have been for a long time now. I hate to be the one to tell you this, but at some point, you have to know the truth before you go and make the big mistake of marrying Nadia Thomas.

I understand that y'all have a baby girl together by the name of Melody. But according to my resources, I don't think that baby is yours.

You see, I work at the Marriott Hotel Downtown around Canal Street. I work in engineering department and I have access to all of the rooms.

I saw her come into the hotel a few times to get a room. She never came alone though. She always be with a tall, muscular and dark-skinned man with dimples. Sometimes they would come together; and sometimes he will leave the room key for her at the front counter. I wasn't sure who the man was. So, I took it upon myself to do some searching. The man name is Evan Jenkins.

After doing my homework, I found out that he was your father. I wasn't sure the reason why they would be getting hotel rooms, until I got a call about a running toilet in their room. When I got there to fix the issue with the toilet, they were both half dressed. After my work was done, I left their room, and I went into the adjoining room. I listened in on their conversation.

They had sex. I heard all the moans and noises from the room next door. After they were done, I could overhear Evan saying something about he didn't want any more outside kids. Nadia said that their child getting older and becoming expensive and the money that he was sending wasn't enough.

Now I am not saying that Evan is the real father of your daughter, Melody, but from their conversation, it seems that way; unless Nadia have another child that you don't know about.

Along with this letter, you will find some hotel receipts with both their names on them, and also some adoption papers. I will advise you to get a DNA done on that child asap. I am sorry to have to tell you this, but I hate to see good people get messed over. I know the feeling. Trust me; Me and you got more in common than you think. And soon, everyone will know. Take care and get that child tested. And think twice before marrying Nadia. She ain't who what you think she is."

    That was the end of the letter. Mark sat back on the sofa, confused. He hoped like hell that this was some sick ass joke. But after seeing those hotel receipts with both his father and his fiancé name on them, he knew that this is official; they were both having an affair with each other behind his back. No wonder his father didn't want him to rush into marriage. He wanted Nadia for himself! This was the ultimate betrayal from his father. He didn't want to blow his cool just yet. He decided to get the yellow pages and make a phone call.

"DNA Testing Center, how may I help you?" the receptionist answered.

"Hi, I have a question. I would like to get a DNA test done for my daughter. Do you except walk ins or do I have to make an appointment? I would like the get it done as soon as today if I can ma'am."

"Yes sir. You can come in today but I must warn you, because you will be a walk in, patients with appointments will be seen first. Would you like to make an appointment or still come in today?"

"I can come in today. I'ma be down there in a minute. Thanks ma'am". He hung up. Mark didn't need to hear anything else. He got his daughter dressed and they were headed out the door.

****

He made it to the DNA Center on St. Charles Ave in no time. He checked in with the front desk and was told to have a seat until his name was called. He sat there and watched his baby girl sleep. He prayed that she was his. He grew angry all over again just the thought of his own father fathering his baby girl; let along sleeping with Nadia. His name was called. The doctors swabbed bout their mouths and told him that the results will be in in one week. This will be the gut wrenching week of his life. Those results will either make or break him.

****

Shante' decided to stop by Danny's apartment in mid-city to pay him a visit. She'd been calling his phone but each time, it goes straight to voicemail. Usually she's against popping up at people's house, but she was getting worried about her best friend.

She rang the doorbell. Just then some half naked woman answered the door.

"Umm, hey. Is my brother Danny there?"

"Yeah he sleep and you are?" That chick had such a nasty attitude.

"Well if I asked is my brother there, that must mean I'm his sister, right?"

"First of all, lose the attitude."

Shante' was about to give this rude ass chick a piece of her mind until Danny appeared in the doorway.

"Man look out and what I told you 'bout answerin' my fuckin' door like you live here and shit? I'm sorry 'bout that sis. These hoes ain't got no manners."

"Yeah I see that."

The chick didn't respond. She just rolled her eyes and went into the bedroom and closed the door.

"I'm sorry for just poppin' up at cha crib but yo peanut headed ass had me worried. Why you ain't been answering yo phone bro?"

"Man, nigga had a lot on his mind with this Benny Jr. situation. I needed to clear my head; and in the mean-time, get some pussy." Shante' slapped his arm.

"Hot ass. When you was gon' tell me that you was fuckin' with Jovita? You know that hoe ran through. Why you even laid up with that nasty heffa? Yo ass better get checked."

"That shit only happened twice. I strapped up the first time but I was full out that liquor when I fucked with her again. Now lil man my son and shit. Shit crazy. He doin' alright though. I been up there to check on him plus Benny been keepin' me updated. I'm glad my lil' man pulled through ya dig. That shit could have gone left for real. So how you been holdin' up since all that bullshit went down with Frank and that hoe Fancee? Y'all cool or what? That bitch need to be in a crazy house somewhere sis. Frank really did a number on her ass. Glad that nigga somewhere rotten." If Shante' didn't kill Frank, Danny damn sure was in line to put him out of his misery after what he did. He guess that good pistol whippin' that he gave him wasn't enough.

"I wouldn't say we best friends or nothin' like that but I do check on her. You know I got a soft heart for hurt people D. I even suggested that she talk to someone about her problems and the things she endured as a child. She been through a lot. Frank really fucked that girl life up. She got a better chance at life now that his ass is gone. She will be just fine with a lil' help."

"Sis, you really a good person. I know some muthafuckas would have put a bullet in her head after that shit she pulled. But you right; she only knew what Frank showed and taught her. Can't fault her for havin' his fucked-up ways. You probably the only person she got now. Keep checkin' on her sis. Get her right."

'I'ma try. But she gotta' want and welcome the help."

"Yeah I feel ya. I knew it was somethin' I had to tell you. I wanted to run somethin' by you a while back but I forget and the shit with Benny Jr. threw me off track. What's going on with Jeremy? Man, word on the street is."

Danny ran all the latest rumors about her brother in law to Shante'. By the time he was finish talking, her mouth was wide open.

CHAPTER 21:
LOST & FOUND

Today was the day. Once he opens the letter from the DNA Testing Center, all things could change.

Mark sat the letter on the table. He rubbed his hands today and covered his face. "Here we go."

He opened the letter and read the results. A smiled appeared across his face. He hurried up to put on his clothes. He grabbed his daughter's diaper bag, along with her and her car seat plus an envelope to take to the post office before he dropped Melody off at her grandmother's house. He hoped she was home.

****

"Hey G-ma, you mind keepin' a quick eye on Melody while I go make a run right quick?" He decided to go shopping for his suit. He was due to get married in in 5 months.

"Sure, my baby. Did she eat yet?" Ask Nadia's grandmother.

"Yes ma'am. I will be right back. Daddy loves you." He gave his daughter a kiss and was on his way.

****

He was jamming Q93 while driving to Men's Warehouse for his suit. He decided while he was out suit shopping, he might as well grab something to eat and get a haircut.

Once he picked out his suit, he took it to the cleaners right up the street from the men's store. To kill time, he went to grab a bite to eat. The lady at the cleaners told him that it would be only an hour before his suit is ready for pick up.

He was sitting in the restaurant, day dreaming about how good he will look to Nadia when she sees him in that suit. All his family members and friends will be there, and most of all, his precious baby girl. He loved his family so much. He couldn't wait for the big day.

It only took him 20 minutes to eat. He had more time to kill so he headed uptown to the barbershop. Once done, he made his way back to the cleaners and picked up his suit. He placed the suit carefully on the passenger seat and drove off.

****

Nadia, Shante', Darlene and Gina were all at David's Bridal shopping for her wedding dress. Their wedding was coming up in 5 months and she was pressed for time. She'd been trying on dresses for the past 2 hours. Everyone was beat and ready to go.

"Girl would you please pick a dress so we can get the hell outta' here. I'm so damn hungry, my stomach touchin' my back and shit." Shante' was ready to go.

"Girl you can't rush perfection. I gotta' make sure I look good on my wedding day. You know yo brother picky. And since y'all know what I'm wearing, none of y'all bitches better not try and upstage me on my big day. I'ma go with the 7th dress 'cause it make my ass look fatter."

They laughed and helped her pick out the rest of her things she needed. She decided on a small ceremony. They were saving for another house and possibly, another baby. They got the details about when her dress will be ready and headed out the door.

"Shante' before you drop me off, can you stop at Rally's right quick? I ain't cookin' shit tonight. My damn feet hurt."

"Cool. I might as well grab somethin' while I'm there too." They got their food and she dropped Nadia off at home.

****

"Baby, I'm back, where you at? I got 'cha somethin' to eat." Nadia called out for Mark but got no answer.

"And why you got this TV up so loud? You gon' be deaf before you make 30."

She walked to their room to put the bags in the closet. She placed her purse on the nightstand and noticed that Mark had a freshly pressed suit laid across their bed. On top of the suit, was a life insurance policy.

"What the hell?" As she read through the pages, she noticed that it was updated a week ago. She saw that Shante' Marie Jenkins was now the sole beneficiary. 100%.

"What the fuck? This nigga…., OH MARK! Where the fuck you at?" She was furious. Why would he take her off his policy and replace her with Shante'? She was the mother of his daughter and his soon to be wife. She was throwed off by this. He had her all the way fucked up.

She yelled for Mark again while turning down the living room TV volume.

"Mark, I know you hear me callin' you!" She thought she heard the car running, so she put the TV on mute. The noise was coming from the garage. With the policy in hand, she headed for the garage.

Just as she thought, Mark was sitting in the car with the engine running. There was so much smoke that she could barely breath.

"Mark, um we need to talk about this damn insurance policy. And why the hell you sittin' up in here with the car runnin'?" She started fanning through the smoke. She grabbed the driver door handle but the door was locked. She tried all the other doors but they were locked too.

She banged on the class to alarm Mark, but he didn't move.

She yelled, "Oh my God MARK, Baby open the door." He still didn't move.

She picked up a hammer that was on the shelf in the garage and she broke the passenger side window. She reached inside, unlocked the door and turned off the engine.

She tried to shake him awake but he wasn't budging. "Baby get up, get up." He had something in his hand. It was an empty pill bottle with no label.

"No, no, no. Mark what did you do?" She ran into the living room and called for an ambulance.

"Please hurry, he's not wakin' up. I think he took some pills." The dispatcher told her that ambulance will be there in 5 minutes.

****

About 30 minutes after Nadia called 911, the place was swarmed with cops, an ambulance and crime lab. Mark was pronounced dead on the scene. They ruled his death a suicide due to the empty bottle of pills that was found, but they will have to get further information from the autopsy. Carbon Monoxide could have also played a part in his death.

Nadia was shaken up. The police were trying to ask her questions for the past 20 minutes, but she didn't respond. She was still in shock.

"Ma'am, we are sorry for your loss. We've searched the premises for more evidence in your fiancé's death, and we found this. We think he had it in his other hand, but once he died it slipped from his grip." Said the police officer.

"What's this?"

"It appears to be a suicide note ma'am. In most suicide cases, there's usually a note left from the victim. Here, take a look at. I think you will get your answer as to why he took his own life."

Once they were finish picking up Mark's body and speaking with Nadia, they left the scene. Nadia was left all alone, wondering what happened. They were getting married in a few months. She thought that they were happy. She broke down in more tears.

"Mark, why baby?" She remembered the note that the officer handed her. She needed to know what was the cause of all of this. She needed answers:

To my amazing, beautiful, sorry excuse for a woman, my fiancé Nadia. The day I first laid my eyes on you, I knew you was the woman I wanted to spend the rest of my life with. You gave me happiness; and I thought you gave me a daughter. It's funny; the day I asked you to be my wife, my father was so against it. He even tried to talk me out of it; and I never understood why. Until now.

Was he worth me losing my life over Nadia? I was a good man to you. You and Melody didn't want for shit. I made sure that all of your wishes, wants and needs were fulfilled. There was nothing is this world that I wouldn't do for you. I gave you my heart, my love, my body, and my ring. And you took all of that away from me. So now I am taking from you.

I know by now that you've gotten this suicide note, along with insurance policy. That's right. I left everything to my sister Shante'. I got it changed a week ago. The day I got word about you and my father, I got a DNA test done on Melody. And guess what? I'm not the father! I'm not sure who is here father, but it's a strong possibility that it's my very own father. My father. My trifflin' ass, low down ass father. It was bad enough that he took my mama through hell, and had another outside kid with Joyce; And yes, Tony is my brother. I found that out too. Now he's the father of my so-called daughter; which is probably my sister. My baby girl Melody. I hurt for her the most.

To save my family the trouble, I got a haircut and I got the suit pressed and ready for my funeral. It's almost time for my big day! From a wedding to a funeral; all thanks to you and my father. So when you see me laid out in that chrome coffin, don't shed no tears for me. Save 'em! Don't go puttin' on no show either; fallin' all in the coffin and shit. Because YOU put me there. I want you to always remember that. If the guilt of what you've done don't eat you up, your conscience sure will. I loved you, and you killed me.

To my beautiful daughter Melody. Baby, I am so sorry. I loved you since the day I found out you existed. You were the light of my life. No matter what type of day I was having, you made it all better with that beautiful smile and those cute babies coos you would make every time you saw my face. Just know that this wasn't your fault. I hope one day when you get older that you will forgive me. No matter what, you will always be my baby girl.

Mark had found out about her and Evan. Instead of feeling guilty, she was more concerned about how he found out.

She tore up the letter and made the phone call that she dreaded.

"Hey, mama Pamela. It's about Mark."

After she told them what happened, all was heard were screams in the background.

CHAPTER 22:
FAREWELL M.J.

It was Friday morning, the day of Mark's funeral. A day that no one will ever forget. The day Shante' found out that her little brother took his own life, was the day that a piece of her had died with him. She never thought in all eternity that she would be burying her baby brother so soon. He'd left her in charge of the funeral. Although it was hard, she had to pull herself together. She needed to be strong for the rest of the family.

The funeral was starting at 11am and the viewing of the body was for 10am. She wanted to be there ahead of time to make sure that everything would be in order. She wanted her brother's funeral to be error free. She had to get dress and head over to her mother's house so she can ride in the limo.

"Good morning Ms. Jenkins. How are ya this mornin'?" The neighborhood mailman was putting mail in the box when Shante' was about to head to her car.

"I wish it could say it was a good day. I'm buryin' my lil brother Mark today."

"I'm so sorry to hear that love. You and your family are in my prayers. So sorry for your loss."

"I appreciate it. I'll take my mail. Might as well put it in the house now." She got a few junk mails and a big manila envelope addressed to her. In place of the return address was a smile; no address.

She placed it on her living room table and headed back out the door.

****

The Jenkins family limo pulled up at the church at a quarter to 10 for the viewing. There were so many cars in the church parking lot. Some people even parked on the median, or as they say in New Orleans, the Neutral Ground.

There were so many people in attendance to say their final farewell to Mark. He was loved by so many people. His old high school basketball team were there; even the few staff members showed up, along with a host of family and friends.

Shante' and her mother exited the limo first; followed by Nadia with Melody in tow, Evan, Gina and Nadia's grandmother. They all walked inside to church to see Mark before the funeral start.

Mark was in deed laid out lovely. He had on the same suit he picked himself from Men's Warehouse. Shante' made sure he got a fresh haircut and his nails were neatly trimmed. As he wished, she purchased an all chrome coffin with gold handles. Mark was looking sharp!

As soon as Nadia and Pamela laid eyes on Mark, they started the flood gates of tears. Nadia laid her head on his said. "I'm so sorry baby. Please forgive me." No one seemed to catch on to what she was saying; everyone but Shante'. She gave Nadia the side eye. What did she mean by forgive her? Why would she need forgiving? She made a mental note to herself that she will question Nadia about it. Right now, she had to grief for her brother.

It was almost 11am; the start time of the funeral. The family was asked to wait outside. They will be coming in last. The family said a quick prayer and was led into the church by the pastor. The funeral services started. It was harder on her than she thought, but Pamela held it together for her family. Everyone said their final goodbyes.

After the funeral, everyone got together and headed by Pamela and Evan's house for the repass. There was music, food and fun. They wanted to celebrate the life of Mark. No more tear drops. He was a good person and he lived a great life.

Mark Christopher Jenkins will always and forever be loved and missed.

****

Chad called Shante' up and see if she wanted to have dinner at Red Lobster. She agreed but she let him know that she was with her sister Gina. She was taking Mark's death pretty hard.

"That's fine, she invited too." Chad wanted to treat them both to dinner. They met up at Red Lobster in Metairie around 8pm. This will be Gina's first-time meeting Chad. She heard so many good things about him.

"Gina, this is Chad; Chad, this is my lil' sister Gina." Shante' introduced the two.

"Finally, nice to put a name with a face. Good job sis. He's a handsome one!"

"Hello Gina. It's finally nice to meet you." They shook hands and headed inside the restaurant. They got a seat at the bar.

"So, tell me Chad, how did you meet my sister?" Shante' almost spit out her drink she Gina asked that question. "You ok sis?"

"Yeah I'm good. Me and Chad met at a party."

"I asked Chad, not you." They laughed.

"Well it's true, we did meet at a party. She was sittin' all alone in the corner; so, I decided to go holla' at her. I was delighted by her beauty."

"And her booty." Gina added. "Oh, you got jokes ha sis?" Shante' laughed it off. Her sister was such a comedian.

"Hello, I'm Wendy. I'll be your waitress. Can I start you guys off with 3 waters?"

"Make that 4." A young lady with blonde shoulder length hair took a seat beside Chad.

"Why the long faces?"

"And who might you be?" Gina gave her the stank face.

"Oh, I'm sorry. I forgot to introduce myself. Hi, I'm Nedra. Chad's wife."

****

Tony pulled up to his mother's house because he had a lot of unanswered questions. He went to the funeral to pay his final respects to Mark. Just a few days ago, he found out that Gina was indeed his half-sister. By now, he'd already fallen in love with her. He knew they would have to break things off. But that was easier said than done.

He used the spare keys he had to Joyce's house. She was laying on the sofa, knocked out. He saw that she had been drinking. There were wine bottles all over the living room. Here hair was in a disarray and she still wore her night clothes from a few days ago. This is not like Joyce. She always kept up with herself.

"Ma, get up. We need to talk; like right nah." He shook her leg to wake her up.

"What is it son?" She got up, wiping her mouth of drool.

"Mama, why did you lie to me about my daddy? First you told me he was dead, then you said he was a dead beat. Not to mention, you told me you had no idea that man was married before you got pregnant with me. And you had me believing that you really didn't know this man had a family. But the other day, the truth came out. All this time I had siblings and a daddy out 'chea, and you decided to hide it from me and lie about it. Even if he was married, you could have told me about him Ma. But you lied. You didn't do it for me, you did it because you wanted Ms. P's husband. You want that woman's life. What type of game you playin' ma?"

"Son, you are young and you wouldn't understand. So, this here ain't even up for discussion. How was the funeral?"

"It was a funeral. How else is it supposed to be? Mama, this shit is messin' my head up. This whole thing been too heavy on my chest. And Gina. Man, I'm fallin' in love with a woman I can't even be with; all thanks to you. Keepin' secrets. Shit like that always backfire ma."

"I know you in your feelings' and shit, but watch your damn mouth in my house. Regardless what happened, you still gon respect me. Ya' understand?" Joyce wasn't going to tolerate disrespect from her son; even though he was angry at her actions.

"She is ya sista'. So you might as well fall ya ass right back outta' love with her. 'Cause that relationship is kaput! Ain't none of that incest shit happenin' over here."

"Mama I wish you would have told me this a long time ago."

"Well I am tellin' ya now! Let her go son. You can't be with her; and that's that."

Tony laid his head on the back of the sofa and closed his eyes. He knew the relationship was over; but he couldn't just turn off his feelings for her like a light switch. This will take time.

"Damn."

****

Chad had been blowing Shante's phone up since she stormed out of the restaurant after learning that he had a wife. That he failed to mention, of course.

"Shante' please pick up the phone baby. Let me explain."

That was voicemail number five.

"Maybe you should hear him out sis. Give him a chance to explain himself. I mean, maybe there's a reason he didn't tell you he was married. You wouldn't know unless you talk to him. Maybe they are not even together anymore." Gina was giving Chad the benefit of doubt. Even though she'd just met him; he started to grow on her in that short time. She can always feel good vibes from people.

"Girl look, whether he with her or not, he still failed to mention that he was married. He didn't give me the option of choosing to be with me him or not. I'm a very understanding person sis, you of all people know that. But I am sick of the secrets. I had enough of that shit with..." Just, forget it. Drop it. I will talk to him when I'm good and ready and now, it's not the time. Too much shit happening all at one time. I'ma give him a call when I cool off."

BUMP! "What the hell?" Someone rear ended Shante'. "Today is just not my fuckin' day!" She pulled her car to the side and turned on her emergency flashers.

When she looked in the rearview mirror, she saw that it was an off-white Nissan Maxima, with eye lashes on the head lights. "Girl you see this shit? Can't be nothin' but a bitch driving that type of shit. That hoe better have some fuckin' insurance. Or Ima snatch them lashes of her car and off her face."

"You mean, his face." Gina said. "That's a damn dude Shante'."

"Girl." Was all Shante' could say.

"That's a pretty ass dude. Damn."

Gina pulled out her cell phone to call the police to report the accident, while Shante' gathered her paperwork and stepped out of the car.

"Oh, my lawd, I am so sorry boo. I stepped on the brakes all late and shit. Everybody in the car alright though?" The driver of the Nissan was showing concern. This put Shante' at ease. Some people tend to be assholes; even if they caused the accident.

"It's just me and my lil sister; and we both fine. Thanks for askin'. You straight too?"

"Yeah I'm good girl. I got insurance and I can pay for whatever damage I caused."

"I appreciate that. My sister called the police so they should be here in a few. Let's switch information and I gotta' take some pictures. I'm Shante' by the way." She extended her hand for a handshake.

"Cute name. And I'm Tracy. Pleased to meet you."

CHAPTER 23:
REARS ITS UGLY HEAD

It has been a month since Mark was laid to rest. Everyone was finally getting bad to their life. Nadia was still having a hard time dealing with his death, but she had to be strong for their, well, her daughter. She still didn't mention Mark's suicide note to Mark's family. And although Mark left everything to Shante', she still looked out for Nadia and Melody. They were family and that's what family do. Nadia decided to move out of the home they shared and moved back in with her grandmother. She didn't want to live in that house, with so many memories. Not to mention, where her fiancé committed suicide.

Gina and Jeremy still have yet to work things out. Jeremy pleaded with her to come home and said he would get help, but Gina knew better. He sang that same song before; only to go back into his old ways after a few weeks. She wanted and needed better for herself. Jeremy was not the man for her. After finding out that Tony was her brother, she decided that it's best that they just try to remain friends. It would be hard but in due time it will work itself out. She still missed him though. He made her feel good about herself; treated her like she was the only woman in the world. Only to find out that it's her half-brother. Life always have a way of throwing a wrench in your plans. Like everything else, she will get over it.

As far as Shante' and Chad, she decided to hear him out. He didn't mention his wife because there was nothing to mention. They had been separated for over 3 years now; still pending divorce. Nedra had no intentions on getting back with him. She just wanted to make his life a living hell. Every woman he came in contact with, she ran them away. Shante' could understand his point and reasons for not bringing her up. But still, keeping the fact that you are married in the dark wasn't acceptable. They got over it. She decided to take things slower until his divorce was final. But they remained in contact.

Pamela and Evan sought counseling. Their marriage wasn't where it should be, but they were working on it.

Pamela decided to throw a get together. The past 2 months had been too stressful for everyone; especially Marks death. She informed every one of the time and location of the get together. Instead at having it at home, she decided to have it at Audubon park. They rented a pavilion and a spacewalk for the kids. Family, friends, food and fun.

****

It was Saturday, the day of the get together. The kids were jumping in the space walk and playing on the playground. The guys had a spades games going and the women were gossiping, as usual.

"Girl this my shit." One of the ladies got up and started doing Da Bunny Hop. The other ladies and a few kids joined in as well. They were getting down! It felt good to see everybody having a good time, laughing and smiling. This was much needed.

****

Cigarette lit, drank in hand, jeans shorts, BeBe shirt, white Nike and rocking shades. Tracy sat in the car, peeping the scenery.

"Jeremy, I know you see me callin' you, nigga. Answer the phone. I see your bitch. Since you wanna duck a bitch, it's time she found out about us." Beep, beep, beep.

There was an incoming call. It was Jeremy. "Tracy, I swear to gawd, if you open yo' fuckin' mouth, bitch I'ma' put a bullet in ya' ass and throw yo' ass in the lake. Try me bitch." Jeremy warned. He was headed to the park to try and convince Gina to come back home. He didn't need Tracy fucking things up with her. He was already in the dog house, and Tracy was about to make the shit worst!

"You know I don't take kindly to threats. This ain't all about you boo. I got some other shit to settle with the Jenkins. So ride the fuck out nigga and suck out my ass." "Click!" Tracy hung up in Jeremy's face.

****

"Hey boo, I didn't know you knew my people." Shante' spotted Tracy walking towards their pavilion. "Thanks for getting my car fixed too."

"I said I would, wouldn't I?" Tracy was annoyed.

"Oh, well excuse me honey." Shante' walked off and joined the rest of the party.

"Umm, hey. Gina, right? Can I talk to you for a minute?" Tracy pulled Gina to the side to have a "chit-chat".

"Yeah, Shante's sister. I remember you from the accident. What's up?"

Look, I don't know how to come out and say this, but…"

"GINA!" Jeremy came storming towards Tracy, and landed a punch, right to his face.

"Didn't I warn you muthafucka. Stay the fuck away from my family. Crazy ass stalker!"

By now, everyone was watching the scene. Tracy was on the ground, holding his face.

"Oh, I got chu nigga. Believe THAT!" He stormed back to his car and came back with some papers, a small folder and his cell phone. He walked pass the crowd and went straight for the DJ section.

"Where the mic at? I got somethin' I gotta say!" He didn't even wait for the DJ to hand over the mic. Once he laid eyes on it, he snatched up from the table and hit it twice.

"Turn the volume up. Mic muthafuckin' check. I'ma need for Ms. Pamela Jenkins, Gina and Jeremy Roberts to come to the front please. Or not. You can hear me from where ya at." HE gave the mic back to the DJ. He didn't need a mic. He mouth was big and loud enough. He just needed to get everybody's undivided attention.

"I know many of y'all don't know who I am. First off, my name is Tracy; Tracy Douglas. And I'ma need y'all full and undivided attention."

He made his way to the front of the eating table. Pamela was his first target.

"Hi, Pamela. How you been? You remember me?"

"I have no idea who the hell you are, but you got about 2 seconds to leave or I'ma throw you out this park my damn self."

"Aww, it that the way to treat your son?" Tracy cocked his head side-ways and started spinning the mic; waiting on Pamela to close her mouth.

"What you mean, your son? My mama has one son and he is deceased. Maybe you showed up at the wrong party. But they got about 3 family reunions going on out here. Maybe you outta' go over there and check ya family tree, 'cause we don't have another brother." Shante' had to let that be known that Mark was the only boy her mother had.

"Oh really? Honey, what do you know? Or, what DON'T you know? Oh, mommy dearest didn't tell y'all her little throw-back secrets? I was the son she gave up for adoption, a very long time ago. That's right. Again, my name is Tracy Douglas. She got pregnant with me when she was only 16. My daddy didn't want me; and I guess she didn't either. I went from foster home to foster home. I've been raped, abused, left for dead and even homeless. You name it, I went through it. I rather you had me aborted than to leave me in the foster care system. But you did. You never tried to look for me; never checked on me. NOTHIN'! Good thing my grandmother, your mother, Belinda checked in on me from time to time. But you just gave me away; and all because my own daddy didn't want you. He left you big pregnant, and you took it out on me. So here I am. I went through leaps and bounds to find you, Mommy. Tt didn't take too long though; thanks to Aunt Fay. As long as I promised to feed her drug habit, she made sure to keep me updated with my mama side of the family. She told me that my mama got married and had 3 more kids. Little ole' me was signed away and forgotten. Well, here I am." Tracy did a little spin around.

"Mama, say somethin'. Is what he sayin' true? Is this what Aunt Fay meant by your secrets?" Shante' had tears in her eyes. She couldn't believe that her mother had another child; and she acted as if he never existed.

"Shante', baby, I was young. I didn't know how to raise a child. My first love left me high and dry. And my mama said I couldn't keep a baby in her house. I didn't want to abort it, so I decided to give it up for adoption. I'm sorry baby. I buried that part of my life a long time ago."

"But how can you forget about your own flesh and blood, Ma? You can't just bury that part of yo' life. I am SICK of all these damn secrets in this family!"

"Come on sis, let's just go." Gina grabbed her sister's hand.

"Not so fast baby sis. I saved the best for last."

He untucked the piece of paper that he had under his arm, and the envelope. He pulled out his birth certificate and gave it to Pamela. Shante' took a peck and sure enough, Pamela's name was listed as the mother. The father's name was blank.

"Gina baby, look. I love you. I love you so much. Let's just go home and work this out baby." Jeremy was on his knees in front of Gina.

"Blah blah bullshit. Jeremy, you so full of shit. You wanna' beg her now after ya' been slappin' her all upside her head for as long as y'all been married. Save that drama."

"And how the fuck would you know that? How do you even know my husband?" Gina was all ears.

"Oh sweetie, trust me, we got a lot in common and we are very much connected for life. And soon, you will know what I mean. Your husband, Jeremy, we met at the gym. Let's just say, it went "beyond" a few training sessions. Your hubby over here, he got a taste for boy pussy too. Yes honey, I been fuckin' your husband; and for a little while now. Nothin' against you my dear. Blame our mammy over there. She's the one behind all of this. I wasn't just gonna' let her live out her life knowin' she threw me away. I been around; hidin' in the shadows. Watching my "family" live on this fake ass 7th Heaven life, while I had to raise myself in this fucked up ass start foster care system. I had to sell my ass just to get by after I ran away from my last foster parents house. I been on my own since. This world wasn't kind to me. The world fucked me; so, I fucked it back. And your husband." Tracy opened the envelope and let all the pictures hit the ground. All of him and Jeremy engaging in all sorts of sexual activities. He even had photos of Jeremy with a dildo up his ass. There was nothing he could say. He just stayed there on his knees, with that dick look.

"You, sorry ass nigga! What, you gay now? You so busy takin' dick up ya ass. That's why you barely fuckin' me? I can't believe this shit! SLAP!" Gina was going off!

"Let's get the hell outta' here. I done had enough of this bullshit." Shante' grabbed her sister and took her to her house. Gina cried the whole ride home.

"I'm so sorry sis. It's not your fault." Shante's tried to console her baby sister. She didn't know what to say. Finding out her own mother abandoned a child, now her brother in law was having an affair with a man?

"Wait, come to think of it. I think that lil finder binder shit was all a part of his little plan. Dirty muthafucka. He been following our family all along."

When Tracy threw the pictures on the ground, Shante' saw that he was also at Gina's birthday party. Now he showed his face, just to cause trouble. Shante' needed to put a stop to this; and fast. Her family was falling apart. Too many lies, betrayal and way too many secrets. This had to end.

CHAPTER 24:
ONE-TWO-THREE BLOWS

Gina has finally decided to return to her home. She'd kicked Jeremy out and got a temporary restraining order against him. He couldn't come within 100 feet of her. She loved having the house all to herself. She was at piece. Well, sort of.

Lately, Gina hasn't been feeling too well. She went to the drug store and got some over the counter meds, but nothing helped. She was always sleepy and couldn't hold down any food. The only thing that seems to agree with her stomach were pineapples. She also noticed that she haven't gotten her period last month.

She went into her medicine cabinet and retrieved a pregnancy test that she purchased months ago. She checked to see if there was an expiration date. It was still good to go. She decided to take it as soon as possible. She needed to know.

She urinated inside of an old mouth wash top that wasn't being used. She placed it on the floor between her legs so she can open the package. Now for the main event: Dipping that stick.
The instructions said to wait 45 seconds for results. One line for negative; two lines for positive. She followed the instructions and waited. Those 45 seconds felt like forever.

"Tss. Here we go." She peeked at the test. Two lines.
"I know you lyin'. Damn Tony!"

****

"Yes, of course. I'm on my way."

Gina called her OBGYN and was told that she can come in today to get a second opinion. She figured the test she took at home was expired. It couldn't be right.

She pulled up to the clinic and walked in. She signed in and waited until her name was called. Shortly after checking in, she was called to the back.

"Congratulations Mrs. Roberts, you're pregnant!" Her doctor delivered the good news. "We are going to get your lab work done today and get you started on some prenatal vitamins. Just get undressed and lay on the table for your pap smear. All of this is normal procedure when pregnant. I'll be right back."

She hadn't had sex when Jeremy in over 3 months. So she knew it was Tony. She needed to give him a call. "Hey Tony, when you get this message, please give me a call. We have a problem. A big problem."

The doctor walked back into the room. "Ok. Now lay back; place your legs in the stirrups and just try to relax. Everything will be just fine."

Once she finished up with her doctor, Gina went to the lab and got some blood drawn. She stopped by the pharmacy to pick up her prenatal vitamins and headed home. She tried Tony's number again but got no answer.

"Please call be back Tony."

****

Shante' was cleaning up and jamming to some music. She decided to rearrange her living room. She got bored with the same look. She went over to her end table to go through a lot of the junk mail that she let pile up.

"Trash, trash, junk, coupons, more trash. Oh, I forgot all about this one." It was the yellow envelope she got the day of Mark's funeral. She never bothered to look at. She decided to look and see who the sender was. There wasn't no name; just a smiley face. She hoped it wasn't one of those annoying surveys that came through the mail.

"What is all of this shit?" When she opened the envelope, there were all sorts of documents. There was a printed email from an anonymous person. It was sent to Mark's email address. Behind the email was a letter addressed to her. It read:

"What's up big sis. If you are reading this, well, it only means one thing: I am no longer here. I clocked out. I made sure to mail this off to you before I took my last breath. I want you to know why I did what I did. I'm sorry for putting you and the family through this heartbreak.

Well. Before I decided to take my life, I wrote a note, hoping that Nadia would find out. Whether she did find it, I'm not sure. It explained why I'm here.

If you haven't read the email that's in the envelope that I sent; I will give you a quick run through of what's on that email. At first, I had no clue who would send me that email, telling me that my own daughter wasn't mine. That's until I got some birth certificate with Mama's name and a dude named Tracy. He was the one that sent me all the proof I needed. He told me that my daughter wasn't mine, but she was fathered, by our father.

Our daddy and my fiancé had been fuckin' around behind my back. This shit didn't just start either. It's been going on sis. She played me for a fool. When I proposed to her, daddy was so against that shit. I never understood why. I mean, I thought he was happy for me. I thought he liked seeing Nadia and I together. I guess that was all a front. I took Melody to get a DNA test. And, well. You'll see the results in the package too. 99.9% not my daughter! Can you believe that shit? I was there when she was born, and I sang to her while she was in her mama's belly. And all this time, she ain't even my seed sis. I couldn't take it. I couldn't live with the fact that my daughter isn't my daughter. And as far as our dad goes, hate is too nice of a word. I wish I knew how to haunt him from this side. Just a few months ago, I was the happiest man in the world. One test, one piece of paper changed all of that. I even got receipts and shit of them checking in the hotels. Every chance they got. I guess when he didn't come home to mama, he was bangin' out my girl. Ain't that some shit?

I bet she was all at my funeral, performing and shit. All fake. She didn't physically kill me, but she killed me. I decided to change the insurance policy. I didn't want that bitch living off of my money. I know you will do the right thing by my daughter. Tell everyone that I love them; and that I didn't suffer. I went peacefully. Do me this favor. Ask about the suicide note I wrote. I know she had to get it. I'm sure the cops searched up and down for evidence in my death.

Well sis, I gotta' go. But one more thing. After you read this letter. Please, and I mean PLEASE, contact Gina ASAP. There is something in this package that she needs to see. This will shake her world, but she gotta' know before it's too late. You know It's bout that sorry ass husband of hers.
I love you. I miss you. Send Gina, mama and my Melody my love. Daddy, tell him to rot. I see you when you get here sis.

Your baby brother,

Lil Mark.
Don't cry for me. I'm alright.

Shante' couldn't think straight. Her mind was all over the place. Her baby brother seemed to talk to her from the grave. That sent chills throughout her body. She read the letter once again. She can hear his voice through his writing.

She looked over the DNA tests, the email that was sent to Mark and the hotel receipts with both her father and Nadia' names on them. Shante' was angry to the 100th power. She was fuming.

"That low down, sneaky bitch." She warned Nadia about her little brother a long time ago. She told her not to hurt him; to treat him right and not to break his heart. She did more than break it. She basically put him in the grave.

She was sick of all the hurt, the pain, the lies, the betrayal and the secrets. Frank took her innocence while her own aunt allowed it. Benny betrayed her with her so-called friend Jovita. Then Danny messed around with Jovita too; which made him Jovita baby daddy. Her father creeping with strippers. Fancee and Frank set her up. Both her dad and Joyce had a 22-year affair, which brings Tony into the picture. Chad kept his wife a secret from her. Gina's husband fucking a man; which turned out to be her long-lost brother that her mother abandoned. Her own father fucking his son's fiancé and got her pregnant. So that makes his granddaughter, his daughter. And that bitch Nadia, betrayed her in the worst way. She broke her brother's heart against her warning. She was against their relationship from the get go, but she blessed their lil relationship after some time. She never imagined that this would be the outcome.

At that point, she didn't trust anybody. Not even her own self. It's like at that very moment, Shante' went into a dark place. She was done caring too much and forgiving so quickly. She was done trying to be strong for everybody else and couldn't even fortify herself. She was done pretending and wearing that mask, as if she was ok. On the outside and from afar, she seemed happy, strong and solid. Inside and close-up, she was broken, destroyed, emotionless and numb. Like a damaged but durable shield.

She wanted to cause some pain and suffering of her own. She was sick of being on the receiving end of everybody's bullshit.

****

Two days had gone by since she received Mark's envelope. She didn't eat, she didn't sleep, nor did she answer her phones. She heard knocks at the door, but she didn't care. Her job called to check on her. Fuck 'em. She quit without notice.

She looked at the clock. It was 11:43am. She grabbed her car keys and was out the door. She was on a mission.

She pulled up to the pawnshop on Veterans. She looked around the shop until she saw exactly what she wanted and waited for someone to assist her. Five minutes later, a salesman approached her. She got straight to the point.

"How much for this 9-millimeter?".

****

"Hello?". It was 1pm in the evening. Gina was taking a nap. She called off work because she was nauseated. Her phone rung three times. The fourth time, she decided to answer. She figured they would keep calling her until she did so.

"Good morning, may I speak with Mrs. Roberts please. This is her doctor."

"Yes, this is she. Did I miss an appointment or something doc?" She was curious about his call.

"Mrs. Roberts, I need you to come into my office as soon as possible. It's very important and I cannot discuss this with you over the phone. I will be here until 4pm. I will be waiting. Please try to make it before then. Goodbye Mrs. Roberts." Click.

"Tssss. Damn." She dragged herself out of bed and freshened up. She threw on some sweat pants and a t-shirt. She didn't feel like getting all dolled up. She looked at her phone again and saw that one of the calls was from Tony.

"Damnit! I'ma call him when I get back. I know this shit better be quick cause I'm tired and this baby whippin' my ass."
She headed to the doctor's visit.

****

"Right this way Mrs. Roberts. Please close the door behind you."

"Yeah so what's this about doc? I thought I wasn't due for another appointment until I turned 12 weeks? Is everything ok? Is my baby ok?" Gina grew worried. The doctor didn't seem his jolly self that day. She sensed that something was wrong.

"First, Mrs. Roberts. How are you feeling today?"

"I'm ok. So what is it you wanted to talk to me about doc?"

"Just a few questions. How many sexually partners have you had in the past 6 months?"

"Why are you askin' me about who I am sleeping with? You know I am a married woman!"

"Please, try to stay calm. I need to know. This is very serious. I need you to be very honest with me. Have you slept with anyone else besides your husband?"

"Look, to be honest with you. Me and my husband are separated. I found out that my husband was having an affair. And yes, I slept with someone else, but it only happened twice. There. I gave you your answer. Now can you please tell me what's going on?"

"I see. Do you happen to know the name of the person that your husband had an affair with? I need names. There's a reason why I'm asking you these questions Mrs. Roberts."

"Yes. His name is Tracy Douglas. That's the guy my husband was seeing and having a sexual relationship with. I found it out recently. Tony Young is the other name. That's who I've been seeing. And he is the father of my unborn child. We had sex a month and a half ago. Around the time that I conceived. Doctor can you cut the shit and tell me what's goin' on? You talkin' in circles and shit, scarin' me. Whatever it is, I can deal with it. Just, give it to me raw."

She was ready to accept any news; she just needed to know what it was. She figured by her getting pregnant by her own brother, that her pregnancy may be high risk. She'd read about cases like this.

"Ok. Are you familiar with Human Immunodeficiency Virus, Mrs. Roberts?"
"No, not necessarily. What is it?" She asked with raised eyebrows.

"Another name for it, is HIV. I'm sorry Mrs. Robert. We've ran your lab tests and the results came back positive. You tested positive for HIV. I'm so, sorry."

Everything else that the doctor was saying was a blur. All she heard was "HIV".
"Thump". Gina passed out on the floor.

CHAPTER 25:
VENGEANCE IS MINE

"Please be home."

Gina stopped by Tony's apartment. Since she found out that he was HIV positive, she wanted to break the news to him in person. She needed to also deliver the news that she was pregnant; with his baby.

She knocked on the door and prayed he was home.

"Who is it?"

"It's me, Gina. We need to talk."

Tony opens the door. "Hey Gina. What 'chu doin' here this early. Everything alright?" It was 6:30 in the morning.

"We have to talk Tony. It's very important."

"Come in." He stepped to the side to let her in. "You want something to drink?"

"No. I just need to talk to you."

"Ok. What's wrong?"

"First, I want to say that I am sorry for my daddy's action. We all was blindsided by the news of you being my half-brother. I know we had to end things; but I would be lyin' to myself if I say I don't have feelings for you. You showed me what it is to feel like a woman; especially after being mistreated for so long. And I thank you for that. You are a good man and hard as this is to say, you will make some woman lucky to have you." Tears rolled down her face.

"I know G. This is hard for me too. I can't just turn off my feelings for you like that. We shared somethin' good and in a snap of a finger, just like that, we had to let it go. Shit been eatin' me up since I found out Evan was my father too. I even stayed away from my mama. She was on some serious bullshit. She went through all that shit just to get Evan for herself. I never knew my own mama could stoop so low."

"I know. My daddy ain't no better; trust me." Gina added.

Well, what's going on? What brings you over here so early?"

She grabbed his hand. This will be hard, but she needed to let him know. "You know that me and Jeremy haven't had sex in over 4 months, right? And we had sex about a month and a half ago, right? Well, last week, I wasn't feelin' too good. I had trouble holdin' down anything I ate; all except for pineapples. I ended up takin' a pregnancy test. And it showed up positive. I had the test in my medicine cabinet for a while so I needed a second opinion. I went to the doctor the same day, and he told me that I was pregnant. Tony, you are the father."

"Aww man." He stood up and started walking back and forth. He was in disbelief. "Gina, you know we cannot have this baby. We blood related. How that's gon look? If that wasn't the case you know I would be overjoyed right now. But we can't bring this baby into this world. Not under these circumstances G."

"I know. I am only 10 weeks. I still have time to... well, you know. I don't wanna' say the word. I agree. We cannot have this baby. But Tony, there's more."

She reached for her purse and grabbed the sheet of paper out of her purse. It was her blood test results. "Look at this."

"What's this?"

"Just read it. I'm sorry Tony. I never meant for this to happen. I just got the news."

He started reading off the paper. It showed that her HIV test results were positive. He read them again to make sure he was reading them correct; positive.

"Hold up. Gina…. you. You got that shit? WHEN THE FUCK DID YOU PLAN ON TELLIN' ME YO' ASS OUT HERE WITH THAT SHIT? So that means I'm HIV positive too? FUCK! NO! Man, this shit cannot be happenin' to me right nah man."

"Tony, I am sorry! I just found out when I went to the doctor. He called me up and told me to come in because of my results. I found out a couple of days ago. I would never intentionally give you HIV! You know I would never do no shit like that! But it's a must that you get tested as soon as possible.

"You fuckin' well right I'ma get tested. You talkin' 'bout you didn't know. How do I know that Gina? You was so quick to give me the pussy. So how I know that shit? You could have been had it! Get 'ya shit and get the fuck outta' my crib Gina. Ever since I started fuckin' with you my life been a livin' hell. First I find out I'm fuckin' my own damn sister, then ya get pregnant and now you gave me HIV! Get the fuck outta' here. Don't ever in yo life show yo fuckin' face around here again." He grabbed her by her arm and led her to the door.

"I'm so sorry Tony. I never meant to hurt you." He slammed the door in her face. She went to her car. She didn't leave right away. She cried on her steering wheel. She knew exactly where she got the virus from. It was from Jeremy. She found out that Tracy was HIV positive. Those words at the family get together replayed in her head:

"Oh sweetie, trust me, we got a lot in common and we are connected for life. And soon, you will know what I mean."

Now she knew exactly what he meant by those words. They were indeed, connected for life.

****

She parked three houses down and waited for her father to leave the house. She rented a black car. She didn't want him to know that she's been following him. She already had his routine down packed. He would meet Nadia out in the open at random restaurants, with their daughter; Melody. They would even meet at those nasty ass motels on Chef Hwy. She had to turn the rental car in tomorrow, so she only had tonight to make moves.

She saw her father get in his car. She started her engine and put the gear in drive. She wanted to be right on his ass.

After trailing her father for 10 minutes, she knew exactly where he was headed; to Nadia's grandmother house. She knew the route so she didn't have to follow so close.

He arrived at his destination in 20 minutes. He parked four houses down. I guess he didn't want anyone to see his car in their parking lot. This had to be the normal routine for him. He knew once her grandmother was sleep, that would be his perfect time to dip through to see Nadia.

"Bastard." She parked across the street. Far enough so he wouldn't notice her. She gathered two envelopes, along with her new Smith & Wesson 9-millimeter and her cell phone. She took a swig of her bottle of Hennessy. She took a final look at her brother's picture before she headed for her father and Nadia.

She had no plans on knocking, so she crept to the back of the house. Nadia's grandmother usually kept her back door unlocked while locking the screen door. Shante' pulled out a thing ruler and unhooked the screen door latch. She as she figured, the back door was unlocked.

The downstairs part of the house was dark, so she had to be careful not to bump into anything. She didn't want to alarm granny and she damn sure didn't want Nadia and Evan catch her. She wanted to catch them off guard.

She crept upstairs and she could hear granny snoring. Good. She wouldn't hear a thing, she thought to herself. She came upon Nadia's bedroom and listened:

"I told you, I can't afford to move out right now. He didn't leave nothing for me nor Melody. Ain't that some shit? He left it all to Shante'. She gave me $5,000 but that money is almost gone. I had to pay my car out because I didn't need my car gettin' repoed. Mark was paying the car note and he was paying all the bills. I couldn't afford to stay in that house even if I wanted to. And the money you givin' me ain't even enough for a one-bedroom apartment in the hood. And ain't no way in hell I'm signing up for no section 8. You think maybe you can talk to Shante' about givin' me more money for Melody? You know how she feels about her niece and you know she gon' break bread when it comes down to Melody. I can just use that money to get a new place. She got well over $75,000 in his life insurance policy."

"Look, why don't ya just move in with me and Pamela. That way you can stack, move around like you want to and be right under the same roof as me and Melody. You can stay in Shante' and Gina's old room. I can talk Shante' into giving you more money for Melody. After 'bout a year, we can move into our own place. We can move to Texas. We ain't even gotta' stay in New Orleans if you don't want to. We can start a life somewhere else. I wanna' be closer to my daughter. She the only thing I got of my son." Evan came up with a solution that would satisfy both him and Nadia. He planned on leaving his wife to be with Nadia and their baby girl.

"Oh, I like that plan baby. I see you thought things through. That's what I'm talkin' 'bout. Yeah, we can leave. I'm 'bout sick of New Orleans anyway. Let's just get this extra money from Shante' and we can go. We ain't even gotta' wait a whole year. We will be ok livin' off your disability too plus find a lil part-time job out there in Texas." She climbed on Evan's lap and started kissing him. He took off her shirt and started kissing on her breasts. They were so caught up in the moment that they didn't hear the door open.

"So, how long has this been going on? Ah ah, don't even try it bitch." Nadia started reaching for her phone once she saw that Shante' had them at gun point.

"Shante, what the hell is goin' on? Put that gun down baby. I can explain everything." Evan had both hands in the air. He saw his daughter but he didn't recognize her. He can tell that she hadn't gotten any sleep. He could smell alcohol on her and her eyes were blood shot red.

She took the 2 rolled up envelopes out of her back pocket. She tossed one over to her father. "Look at it; both of y'all."

"What it this?"

"I SAID LOOK AT IT MUTHAFUCKA!" She snapped.

They both looked over the documents. It was a copy of everything that Mark sent to her. DNA tests, hotel receiepts, pictures, Tracy's birth certificate and even Tracy's HIV test results that he wanted Mark to give to Gina. Nadia covered her mouth.

"I already stuck a copy in mama and Gina's mailbox. I made sure to make you one for you too so you can take it to your grave."

"Oh, my God Shante', please don't do this!". Shante' couldn't believe these two. How could the two people she trusted so much betray her like this? Her heart was beating outside of her chest. With her black & silver, 9 milli-meter Smith & Wesson in hand, she pointed the gun from her and back to him.

"Just shut up! How could you do this to me? To him? How could you hold such a secret when you've witnessed the heart ache and pain that I went through after losing him? He loved you. He would have done anything for you. I told you not to break his heart; but you did and it killed him!", Shante' said with tears rolling down her face. "And you, turning the gun back towards him, "WHY SHOULD I LET YOU LIVE YOU SON OF A BITCH? You are the cause of all this shit that's been goin' on. With all your lies and secrets How could you do this time him? He was your son!

"I was going to tell you but I didn't know how. I didn't mean for this to happen. You gotta believe me. Shante', baby girl please put the gun down and let's talk about this. I am so, so sorry. Let's just please talk about this before you……

POP POP POP!!!

Screams rung throughout the house as she screamed at the top of her lungs as she watched Shante' released 3 rounds into his skull. "OH, MY GOD NOOOO".

POP! POP! Shante' let off two rounds into her back without so much as a blink. She stepped over their dead bodies and placed the manila envelope on the bed. Although she looked over these documents and pictures over 100 times, each time the pain was unbearable. She couldn't believe what she'd done, but it was too late. What happened, happened.

She went downstairs to the kitchen cabinet and took out a wine glass. She knew the place like the back of her hand. She went into the pantry and grabbed a bottle of red wine. She wasn't much of a drinker but after the mind-blowing news and betrayal she'd received, she figured what the hell. She gulped down her drink and poured herself another one.

She gulped down her drink. She knew the neighbors had probably already called the police right about now, but she didn't care. She wasn't running. She figured her life was already over. Too much has happened. She was losing control. She didn't want to live, so she planned on taking the easy way out. Jail wasn't an option for her. Wiping the tears from her eyes, she then turned the gun to herself. "Lord, please forgive me!"

…. POP!

Moments later.

"Nadia, baby what's all this noise I hear down here?

AUGHHHH!" Nadia's grandmother walked in the bedroom and witnessed a blood bath. She saw her granddaughter's body laid across a man's body. She couldn't recognize him. She saw that he saw shot in the face, while Nadia was shot in the back.

"I need to police over here. My grandbaby got shot. I don't think she is breathing. Oh Lawd. Please hurry." She gave the dispatcher her address.

****

"Ma'am, ma'am. Stay with us. Look at me. Tell me your name. Hurry, we are losing her. Stay with me ma'am."

She can hear the wailing of the ambulance. She didn't know what was going on. She heard voices but couldn't comprehend what they were saying. She started to feel cold. She closed her eyes and saw nothing but darkness.

CHAPTER 26:
WHEN IT ALL BOILS DOWN

"Right this way. Please empty everything out of your pockets and place them in the container. Have your ID out as you come through the scanner please. Thank you."

Gina and Pamela were headed to visit Shante'. She was in a coma for over 3 weeks. She recovered from her gunshot wound to the abdomen. She was doing so much better now.

Gina ended up getting the abortion. Her doctor started her medication for HIV. She tried to reach out to Tony, only to find out that he got his number changed. He even moved out his apartment. She thought of him often. She still wanted something type of relationship with him; after all, he was still her brother. After learning of his HIV status, Jeremy committed suicide. Gina couldn't allow herself to shed one tear for him. This was all his fault. He made her life hell on earth. Good riddance.

While Shante' was in the hospital, her best friend Danny and Darlene came to visit. Even Benny came to check in on her. She was still in a coma.

When she finally came to, there were all sorts of get well cards, flowers and balloons through-out her room.

A psychiatrist came to speak with her through-out her stay at the hospital. Although she was charged with the murders of both her father and Nadia, they were seeking the insanity plea; here's why.

Shante' has been suffering from a mental disorder all of her life. Her parents would notice sudden changes in their daughter's behavior. At times, she could be the sweetest, and most fun-loving little girl. But sometimes, she was like Dr. Jekyll and Mr. Hyde. Many night Pamela would cry herself to sleep; hoping that her daughter would someday grow of it. She had to get some help for her daughter. So she sought out help from a psychiatrist.

She wasn't put on any medication right away. Doctors had to make sure that they prescribed her with the correct medication that she needed for her condition. The medicine that they finally prescribed her with, kept her calm and focused. After about 4 years, her mother discontinued her meds because she was starting to coop without them. Or it seemed that way.

12 years ago, after taking out her revenge on Frank, her mother decided to talk to someone about what her daughters encountered. She would bring both Gina and Shante' to speak with a social worker, but only Gina would participate in the sessions.

Shante' didn't think she needed to see a shrink. She never liked seeing her own psychiatrist, let alone a social worker. She felt that way even before the case with Frank. What she did to Frank is what any child would have done. That's what she told her doctor and herself. Her mother, the social worker and the psychiatrist agreed to put Shante' back on her medication. Shante' reverted back to her old ways since that incident with Frank.

Although she refused the counseling, she agreed to taking her medication again. She's been taking it through-out most of her life. This was a secret she would take to her grave. Not even Danny knew of her medication intake and mental disorder. She didn't need people looking down on her or feeling sorry for her. She kept that part of her life to herself.

The medication helped her coop with life. She was still having flashbacks. The medication didn't take away the problem; but they helped her with everyday living.

The day of her brother's death is when she stopped taking her medication. It was all downhill from there. She saw the world as her enemy.

"Wait right here. She will be out in the minute." The Technician said to Gina and Pamela. Seconds later, Shante' came out from the back room.

"Hey my baby. How you doin'? How they treatin' ya in her? You takin' your meds?" Pam stood up and gave her daughter a big hug.

"Yes mama. They make sure I take my meds in here. I am doing ok, considering the fact that...."

"Just thank God that you are still alive. That's all that matters. It could have been so much worst baby. By the Grace of God, you are still here with us. Lord knows we been though too many funerals as it is.
Melody is doing fine. She's at her grandmother's house until we get back. They told us children aren't allow here. We decided to raise her; Gina and me. You know that's what Mark would have wanted. I went to visit your daddy's grave yesterday. I pray you forgive your father someday Shante'. Do you know how better your life will be if you forgive baby? I'm not asking you to forget. I know it's been hard for you these past few months. We all go through betrayal, lies and deceit. But when it all boils down, it's up to you to let go of all that hate in ya' heart. Don't let it eat you alive and weigh you down baby. God gave you a second chance at life for a reason. I know you've done some things and made some bad decisions. Most of them wasn't your fault baby. And no one is perfect. Even broke crayons still color. You will be alright as long as you remember that phrase baby."

"She's right sis. I know it's hard for you to forgive daddy. And we all know that you are one stubborn Scorpio. But all jokes aside, just think about it. It doesn't have to be right now. Give it some time. It was hard for me to forgive him, and Jeremy. But I had to. It didn't change the outcome but I feel a lot better. I would have never thought I would be tryin' to get my life back in order again while being HIV positive. I joined a group of other people that's in the same position as I am. You would have never thought that they were infected. They are still out here, livin' and enjoyin' their lives. It's not the end of the road for me. I know that now. Same for you sis. Just except all the help. We will never stop believing in you. We are family. We all we got." Gina kissed her sister on the forehead.

"I'ma think about it mama. Things just happened so fast and it just seems like a ton of stones were piled on top of me. I needed to release some anger. I watched myself outside of myself. I thought revenge would make me feel better; I still feel the same; numb. But I am glad to still be alive. Thanks for comin' to see me today."

They talked for another hour until visitation time was over.

"Well, we will be back next week to see you baby. We love you so much. Stay strong, pray and make sure you takin' your medicine. This is where you need to be. I rather you here than locked up in some women's prison somewhere. Let these people help you make yourself better so you can come back home to us. Take care of yourself in here baby. Let us know if you need anything. We love you." Pamela and Gina hugged Shante'; they even shed a few tears together.

"I love y'all too. See y'all next week." She watched them leave. She missed them so much, but she knew she had to be there. She wasn't ready nor was she mentally stable to face the world again. Not at this time. She needed to heal and get better.

The Tech walked over to Shante' in the dayroom.

"You wanna stay in here Ms. Jenkins, or go back to your room?" He asked.

"Nah, I don't wanna' be in here with these crazies. I'll go back to my room." They both laughed.

He grabbed the handles of her wheelchair and took her back to her room.

𝒯𝐻𝐸 𝐸𝒩𝒟

ABOUT THE AUTHOR

Shannon Marie Jefferson, also known as Doobie, was born and raised in Uptown New Orleans, Louisiana. After graduating from Walter L. Cohen High School in 1997, she enlisted in the military. U.S. Navy and Army. After being honorably discharged, she decided to return to Louisiana to focus on raising her kids, obtaining a degree and working on her first novel. She has plans on writing short horror stories in the near future.

CPSIA information can be obtained
at www.ICGtesting.com
Printed in the USA
LVOW04s0614230817
546063LV00032B/286/P